Put Your Money to Work

The Private Investors' Guide to Real Estate

Anca Markie

Caline Bruyn

Introduction

Thank you for taking the time to read this book. This book was written because of the wonderful people we have met who want to know how to invest in real estate without working any harder than they already do. Many of you already have your money working hard for you. For others, this is a foreign concept that you would like to explore. Either way, it is something anyone can do. Whether you have a vast amount of wealth or you are looking to take what little you have in a retirement account and create a nest egg to enjoy later in life, this book will help you understand the power of being a private investor in real estate .

First, let's clear up a few things when it comes to terminology. The term *investor* is interchangeable with several other terms, and can become ambiguous. An investor is someone who invests his or her money in some sort of an asset. Investors put their money to work or commit capital in order to gain financial returns. Therefore, for purposes of this book, you are an investor. In the real estate world, you become a *debt partner* or an *equity partner*. Some may refer to you as a *private investor*, or a *private money partner*. Whatever the case, you are a vital part of the real estate partnership, and it is very important that you are knowledgeable and recognize what it is to be a private investor.

An *entrepreneur* is an individual who organizes and manages any enterprise, especially a business, usually with considerable initiative and risk. What we have come to know as real estate investors are, in fact, and in most cases, entrepreneurs.

So, to make things clear for the purposes of this book, we refer to the erstwhile real estate investor as the real estate entrepreneur, which you will often see shortened to a simple REE.

The purpose of this book is to help guide you on the virtues of partnering with a real estate entrepreneur. You will discover what to look for in a good REE, what you should expect and not expect from the REE and your investments, what questions you should ask, and the answers you should anticipate.

Caline and I really enjoyed writing this book. We like to think of it as a travel guide...designed not only to get you to your destination, but to ensure you have a great experience getting there and a great experience once you have arrived.

Use this as a guide. We don't expect you to read it cover to cover, although it may be helpful to do that first. Then go back to those parts that you want to make sure you understand before venturing out in to the world of private investing. Each chapter has a section of frequently asked questions. These come from our experience working with private investors. If you find that you have more questions, please go to our website, www.theprivateinvestorbook.com. Fill in the contact form with your question and we will find you the answer!

After reading the book, if you are so inclined, please provide your feedback, whether you liked the book or didn't. We also want to hear about your experiences with a real estate entrepreneur (good or bad...you don't have to name names!).

Now, begin your journey to becoming a private money partner!

Anca Markie

Caline Bruyn

Legal Notice

The information in this book is designed to provide accurate and authoritative information in regard to the subject matter covered. It is offered with the understanding that the presenters are not engaged in rendering legal, financial, or other professional services. If legal or other expert advice is required, the services of a competent professional should be sought.

CONTENTS

1. The Real Estate Entrepreneur Mindset   1
    - The Mindset
    - Where to Find Real Estate Entrepreneurs
    - Frequently Asked Questions
    - A Word About Crowdfunding
    - Frequently Asked Questions

2. Advantages of Real Estate   11
    - Why Real Estate Returns Are Higher than Stocks, Bond and Mutual Funds
    - Frequently Asked Questions

3. What Kind of Investor Are You?   19

4. The Real Estate Market (Cycle)   28
    - How Do Real Estate Entrepreneurs Read the Market?
    - How the Market Cycle Affects Investing
    - Frequently Asked Questions

5. What Type of Properties?   36
    - Single Family
    - Multifamily Residential
    - Commercial
    - Office
    - Industrial
    - All Those Choices!
    - To Flip or Hold
    - Building Wealth

6. Legal Issues with Real Estate Investments   42
    - Types of Legal Entities
    - The Importance of Formalities

- Land Trusts
- Tax Issues with Real Estate Investments
- Self-Directed IRAs

7. The Debt Partnership   56
    - What You *Should* Expect as a Debt Partner
    - The Private Money Loan
    - Debt Partner Basics
    - Frequently Asked Questions

8. The Equity Partnership   67
    - A Sample Flip Scenario
    - Long-Term Equity Investing
    - The Best Part about Being an Equity Investor
    - Equity Investor Expectations
    - A Quick Word about Syndication
    - Frequently Asked Questions
    -

9. Transparency   83
    - Four Key Factors
    - The Groundwork
    - The Cash Flow or Flip Analysis
    - The Due Diligence
    - Post Closing
    - The "Guarantee"
    - Frequently Asked Questions

10. Case Studies   95

11. A Final Word   101
    - "Inspirational" Quotes

Terms and Definitions
About the Authors

Note

We occasionally use real estate investment terminology that may be unfamiliar. We have included a list of Terms and Definitions in the back of the book to help you learn the "jargon".

Chapter 1:

The Real Estate Entrepreneur Mindset

What I refer to in this book as the real estate entrepreneur or REE is more commonly known as the real estate investor or REI. I believe "entrepreneur" is a more appropriate term, but you will find that most of us continue to refer to ourselves as real estate investors. —Anca Markie

Consider this:

The majority of wealthy people in the world have either made their money in real estate or invested in real estate after they built and operated successful businesses.

Clearly many who wish to be wealthy and financially secure gravitate toward real estate as a means to accommodate those desires. They know to "follow the money."

So while it's understood that there's a strong correlation between real estate and wealth, what's less obvious is that the inclusion of a focused business mindset is what completes the formula. Wealth is the destination, real estate is the vehicle, and a determined, business-minded way of thinking is the fuel. A strong business mentality and approach is the element that ultimately enables successful investing.

Most people who have made their money entirely from investing in real estate did so with a serious "treat-it-as-a-business" attitude, which itself was driven by a healthy entrepreneurial spirit. Generating wealth and achieving financial security through real estate investing truly is a (big) business and must be addressed as such. If it were easy, anybody could and would do it. Most aren't willing to do what's necessary. Those who are tend to prosper.

Successful real estate entrepreneurs have highly developed and activated desires to realize their goals and destinations. They don't allow outside forces to impede. They're open, they search for and embrace all sources of helpful information, and they are incredibly optimistic and devote whatever time necessary to perform all of the due diligence to support their aims and minimize risks. If there are weaknesses or certain areas where they lack knowledge, extra emphasis on those is applied. They seek wisdom from, work with, and partner with those who've already succeeded. As the right work is being done, fear and comfort zones become nonfactors and success becomes likely. Then, most importantly, they **take action.**

Real estate investing is not something that only wealthy people do. In many cases, investing in real estate is how their wealth was created. It should not be treated as a hobby. It is serious business, and understanding that separates those who are currently wealthy and those about to become so from the others.

The Mindset

The mindset refers to how real estate entrepreneurs think. This goes back to the big question *why*. What motivates them? The most successful will tell you it's a passion. But what does that mean? Bill Strickland, author of *Make the Impossible Possible*, offers some clues. He writes: "Passions are irresistible....If you're paying attention to your life at all, the things you are passionate about won't leave you alone. They're the ideas, hopes, and possibilities your mind naturally gravitates to, the things you would focus your time and attention on for no other reason than that doing them feels right."

It's not about the money, but what the money will allow them to do...to accomplish...to pass on to children and grandchildren...to build a legacy...to be philanthropic...to do what they desire.

Whether a real estate–investment company is a single-member LLC or has many employees, the most successful REEs all have one thing in common: it's a business, not a hobby. Any real estate entrepreneur will agree that mindset, just as with any business, is vital. A savvy REE has a strategy and has created systems to build a healthy business that will survive good and bad markets. It is the mindset, and the drive to succeed even through failure, that create the most successful real estate entrepreneurs.

Real estate entrepreneurs have a unique way of looking at real estate. They don't get emotional; they can't get emotional. It all becomes a numbers "pursuit." The deal is based on the numbers: great numbers...great deal. Good numbers...good deal. Bad numbers...well, you get the picture. The only emotion comes from being sensitive to the needs and desires of the REE's partners. REEs want great deals so great profits can be made and shared with the partners.

Now that you understand a bit about the real estate entrepreneur mindset, let's consider where you can find a REE with that mindset.

Where to find Real Estate Entrepreneurs

As a REE, one of the most important steps in building wealth is finding partners. These partners include other real estate entrepreneurs and professionals, real estate attorneys, mortgage bankers, contractors, commercial investors, and private investor partners.

Successful REEs are always building their networks and seeking relationships with other successful people. Here are four ways to locate REEs:

#1. Through your private network.

Talk to your circle of friends and acquaintances, people you work with, and family. Talk to your accountant, and your investment or financial advisor. It's amazing how many people know at least one real estate entrepreneur. Remember—they will likely call them real estate investors.

#2 Local networking groups

One of the ways to meet real estate entrepreneurs is through local networking groups. These may be real estate centric, business groups, or social groups. Some of the more common real estate–centric groups include the REIA (Real Estate Investors Association), ACRE (Association of Commercial Real Estate Entrepreneurs), AOA (Apartment Owners Association), or a host of other similar groups. Find these groups at www.meetup.com and keyword search *real estate investor* or Google *REIA* in your local community.

Many have regular weekly or monthly meetings that are open to guests. I would suggest you go to as many of these meetings as you possibly can. Learn as much as you can about the people who are members of these groups. Listen to the conversations, and introduce yourself. Collect business cards and then start making phone calls. But, don't be surprised if you start getting some calls first!

Your city or town will have a Chamber of Commerce, Rotary and church groups, business networking groups, and other social and business groups that attract REEs.

#3 LinkedIn, Twitter, Facebook

Create Twitter and LinkedIn accounts and search for real estate entrepreneurs, real estate investors, and so on. Join real estate centric groups in LinkedIn. Groups like Multifamily Investing Academy, The Real

Estate Networking Group, Investing in Real Estate, and dozens more offer the opportunity to meet active real estate entrepreneurs. Just as with any other online places you may go, always be careful. These groups do their best to prevent scammers, but a few do slip through every now and then. Always, always, build the relationship first. Get to know the REE and let him or her get to know you.

#4 Craigslist...Really!

You can go to craigslist and observe how many ads there are for "we pay cash" or "seller financing" or "we buy houses"...you know the kinds of ads we mean. Respond to these ads with "I'd like to know more about how you buy for cash." Start conversations with those placing the ads. Look for real estate entrepreneurs that are happy to talk to you. If they don't want to give you the time of day, or don't respond to your contact, move on to the next one.

What you should NOT do.

We don't recommend that you put an ad on craigslist, Facebook, LinkedIn, or other social media advertising that you have money you want to invest in real estate.

There are too many scams out there, and too many people itching to separate you from your money. And, to be honest, no REE in his or her right mind would respond to such an ad, because it may be a scam. Please understand, you will find these ads, and not all of these are fraudulent, but the risk is ever present. Many of these ads may come from legitimate private lenders, but they will always include a website.

Here are some really important tips:

- It's important that you find a credible real estate entrepreneur.
- Look for recommendations from friends, family, acquaintances, and business partners who have invested with a REE or know someone who has.
- Do your due diligence. Once you meet with a REE, ask for references, Google him or her, and ask about the types of deals they've done with their partners and team.
- Check out their websites.
  - Any experienced, credible REE will have a capital funding or equity partner page, if not an entire site devoted specifically to information on the subject of raising capital.
  - If a site asks for your contact information in a landing page, GIVE IT. It's the best way to get the information you need to make an informed decision on investing your money in real estate.

Frequently Asked Questions

Q: Why is knowing the real estate entrepreneur's mindset important to me?

A: It helps you understand what to expect. If a REE has a business mindset, you can expect a professional.

Q: What sort of questions should I ask to get a better feel for a REE's mindset?

A: Start with, "How long have you been in business?" Then follow up with, "What is the primary focus of your business?"

Q: Is it important that I partner with a real estate entrepreneur with goals similar to my own?

A: That isn't always necessary. If a REE is a professional, he or she will want to know your goals and when the property strategy aligns with those goals, they will discuss the investment opportunity with you. That is far more important than whether his or her personal or business goals match yours. The REE's focus is on how can the property exit strategy best profit everyone involved.

Q: I'm looking for a long-term investment that is aggressive, yet sustainable. What type of REE should I be looking for?

A: "Long term" typically refers to sustainable cash flow, which is not the most aggressive investment. But, if the property is distressed and requires repositioning, and then cash flows...that can be the trifecta (although a greater risk) in aggressive profits plus sustainable returns. Talk to your REE to discuss your investment goals.

Q: I'm a risk taker, but I'm tired of losing money in the stock market. Would being an equity investor in real estate give me the kind of returns I'm looking for?

A: Real estate in general is not a high-risk venture . That being said, there are high-risk strategies within real estate investing. If you are looking for fast, high returns, you may want to look for a REE who implements the fix-and-flip strategy.

Q: I've been to several local REI (real estate investor) clubs, but can't seem to find a REE who invests in commercial property. Most of these clubs seem to attract "small time" and part-time entrepreneurs. Where else can I look?

A: We would suggest you look at your local ACRE group, or your local Apartment Owners Association. A good source would be commercial real estate groups in Linked In. Other resources would include talking to your accountant, your investment or financial advisor, your insurance agent, and so forth.

A Word About Crowdfunding

Crowdfund investing could revolutionize how people raise money for their enterprises, but it can also expose unwary investors to financial peril.

Crowdfunding itself isn't new. Many businesses, start-ups, and individual entrepreneurs have raised millions for projects around the world. Equity crowdfunding (a newer concept) turns donors into investors. In 2012, Congress voted in the Jumpstart Our Business Startups (JOBS) Act, which has paved the way for small companies to offer stock (or shares) online. The idea was to stoke job creation by making it easier for entrepreneurs to raise money. Even more recently, real estate entrepreneurs have found that crowdfunding may be an easier way to raise capital for property investing.

This is a monumental shift in the way businesses can raise capital, and with it comes risks. Here are two major risks:

For the entrepreneur—If the funding goal is not met, all capital raised must be returned. Suppose a business needs to raise $1million to cover down payment, closing costs, and due diligence costs and fees on a property. Now, lets say that the first raise obtains $200,000, which is used for due diligence and attorneys' costs. When the business is unable to raise the entire amount, it must all be returned—even the $200,000 already used. Ouch!

For the investor—If the business hits its funding goal but later fails—or, in the case of a REE, the property doesn't profit as expected—the investors could lose part or all of their investments.

You may think, "Well, that's no different from any other kind of investing," and you would be right.

But what we feel is the most important difference between crowdfunding and other means of obtaining private investors is that crowdfunding investments are not built on relationships. You are just part of the "crowd," and as a result, there is greater danger of fraud-related risks.

If you are considering investing through a crowdfunding website, be aware of the rules and regulations...and do your homework!

Frequently Asked Questions

Q: How much money can a business raise through crowdfunding?

A: Up to $1 million a year. That may seem like a lot, but when you consider that the average real estate entrepreneur may need to raise $2 million or more on a single commercial property, crowdfunding would not be the answer.

Q: How much can I invest?

A: Individuals with less than $100,000 in assets or income can invest 5 percent a year or a maximum of $2,000, whichever is greater. Those with higher incomes can invest 10 percent a year, up to $100,000.

Q: Can I get my money back?

A: If the company fails to reach its funding goal, you won't be charged. If the funding campaign succeeds and the business fails later—or, as in the case of a fix-and-flip, the house if foreclosed on—your investment is probably gone.

But here is the good news. In the fix-and-flip, you would be doing the foreclosing and you would have the house—an asset that you can turn around and sell to get at least part of your investment back.

Q: How does the JOBS Act impact crowdfunding

A: Remember that crowdfunding is simply syndicating (see chapter 8) using the Internet.

The JOBS Act was signed into law on April 5, 2012 by President Obama, and is currently under an SEC rulemaking period. The JOBS Act was meant to enable crowdfunding for all investors, both accredited and nonaccredited. Real estate entrepreneurs are only impacted by this act when they open investor pools to both accredited and nonaccredited investors and do not rely on legal structures and exemptions that existed before the JOBS act. It's important that you discuss this with the REE you are working with, if you are investing as a result of crowdfunding.

Chapter 2:

Advantages of Real Estate

You may have heard many times throughout your life that "you can't have your cake and eat it too." I never understood that. Why can't I have my cake, with ice cream and extras, and eat it too? That's what investing in real estate is all about.

This may seem like a very simplistic analogy to real estate investing, but as a REE, I find that using this narrative helps the private investor understand the approach I take. — Anca Markie

Why Real Estate Returns Are Higher than Returns on Stocks, Bonds, and Mutual Funds

Investing in rental property is like eating a 3 layer cake with ice-cream and a cherry on top!. Buying stocks, bonds and mutual funds is like eating a cupcake with the occasional spoonful of ice cream.

When holding real estate (whether residential or commercial), your returns include:

1. Cash Flow from Monthly Rental Income— The first decadent chocolate layer

2. Buying Money— A second layer of vanilla cream

3. Tax-Free Refinancing— A Third layer

4. Appreciation— Frosting on Top

5. Write-Offs— A scoop of rich vanilla ice cream

6. Depreciation—The Cherry on Top

With typical stocks, bonds or mutual funds, your returns include:

1. Appreciation (Capital Gains)— Cupcake

2. Cash Flow from Quarterly Dividend—A Quarterly Scoop of the Ice Cream

Investing is all about getting your money to make you money, but the money can come in many forms. With real estate, the money comes from cash flow, buying money, appreciation, tax-free refinancing, write-offs and depreciation. For typical securities, your money comes in from capital gains and dividend cash flow. So when you read an article that touts historic high returns for stocks over real estate, you need to make sure the real estate returns include all the parts of the "layer cake."

Marlys Harris, *Money* magazine senior editor, wrote:

   "Housing delivered a solid but unimpressive annualized return of 8.6 percent. Commercial property did better at 9.5 percent. The S & P, however, delivered a crushing 13.4 percent."

Selena Maranjian of the Motley Fool penned:

   "The long-term average annual growth rate for real estate is around 5 percent. Per data from Ibbotson, the stock market (as measured by the S & P 500) has averaged 9.7 percent annually between 1926 and August 2010, while long-term government bonds averaged just 5.6 percent."

What part of the hot fudge sundae are Harris and Maranjian talking about with their "8.6 percent" and "5 percent" returns? Though they don't specifically state what they were measuring, I'd guess they are comparing the real estate's frosting (appreciation) to the stocks' frosting (appreciation/capital gains) and stocks' quarterly scoop of ice cream (dividends). I'm assuming Harris and Maranjian's figures left out the most important aspect of rental returns: the cash flow, as well as the rest of the layer cake. When you really want to calculate your real estate returns, you need to factor in all the ways the money comes in.

So, what about the rest of the real estate layer cake?

Cash Flow from Monthly Rental Income
The first decadent chocolate layer

We love to focus on the cash flow. If we were a stock or mutual funds investor, We'd buy dividend funds for the cash flow. But we prefer to make our own dividends, our own cash flow, from monthly rental income. We believe the analysts' figures skip over the returns from rental income, but we bet they have included stock dividend income in their numbers. If you buy rentals right, you should produce rental income at a "crushing 13.4 percent" or better, or at least "9.7 percent annually." And that's with the rental income alone.

Buying Money
A layer of vanilla cream

If you buy one share of a stock, you get only one share. If you buy a rental unit, you can buy one-and-a-half shares for the cost of one share. Or better yet, you can buy two shares or more for the cost of one share. We like to buy money, to buy equity.

We refinanced a property this month. Here are the numbers:

Initial price: $500,000

Rehab cost: $50,000

Total cost: $550,000

Rent: $9750/month (15 units at $650 each)

After Repair Value and Appraised Value after six months of seasoning: $950,000

$950,000 minus $550,000 = $400,000

So you could say we essentially "bought" $400,000 in equity. Now $400,000 of the initial $550,000 investment is a 73 percent gain that took only six months' seasoning. We'll take the 73 percent gain in six months any day.

The thing is, a real estate entrepreneur can fairly accurately predict what the new after-repair value will be before he or she buys a property.

Tax-Free Refinancing
A Third Layer

Let's say you want to pull out some money from your stocks. Well, that would be a taxable event. If we refinance and pull out our equity, we're not taxed. Can anyone say "hallelujah?"

Appreciation
Frosting on Top

Appreciation (capital gains) is the main way stocks get their return on investment (ROI). For rentals, appreciation—which often isn't even factored into the returns—is the added bonus, the "hot fudge on top."

Write-Offs
A scoop of rich vanilla ice cream

Your write-offs from stock investments are extremely limited. You can write off your annual fees and cost basis. With real estate, you can write off property expenses, any related expenses, capital improvements, debt, debt related expenses...is anything missing?

Depreciation
The Cherry on Top

Depreciation is a gift from the government. If I were musical, I'd write a song about depreciation. Make sure your tax accountant knows all about depreciation and contents depreciation. Can you depreciate your stocks, bonds, and mutual funds?

With stocks, most analysts are looking at returns based on price and dividends together to give the "crushing 13.4 percent" or the "9.7 percent annually." But with real estate, your return is based on a lot more. Imagine that the "8.6 percent" and "5 percent" mentioned in the quotes above are only the appreciation returns. Now add buying equity, tax-free refinancing, write-offs, and depreciation gains. And the best part of all—add in the cash flow from monthly rental income. With real estate rentals, investors get to eat the entire hot fudge sundae.

This is why the REE invests in real estate...He or she sees that the benefits far outweigh the pitfalls. You will learn in later chapters that the advantages for you as the private investor can be the same.

Frequently Asked Questions

Q: Why do you invest in real estate?

A: You will get many different answers here. But when we talk to REEs, the most common answer is, *"Because I love it, and in spite of the long hours, I just don't think of it as work!"*

Q: Why should I consider an investment in real estate?

A: Allocating some portion of your portfolio to a direct investment in real estate may provide you with a reasonably predictable and stable level of current income from the investment, the opportunity for capital appreciation, and diversification of your portfolio by investing in an asset class that historically has not been correlated with the stock market in general.

Q: Is real estate investing risky?

A: In a word—yes. But the risk will vary based on the exit strategy implemented. This is why you will want to be sure the REE is backed by a team of trusted professionals with experience in real estate investing and asset management. Any REE that you work with should have the appropriate due diligence framework in place to provide you with the best option for a profitable venture. The REE should do this by painstakingly analyzing each investment, structuring it in a manner where you are not the last one to get paid if a project goes bad. He or she should have an efficient monitoring system, via an asset management team that ensures the project is on schedule and the funds are being used per the offering memorandum that has been shared with you. Please bear in mind that the securities and investments with *any* REE may be high risk, but they may be high return as well. There is always the risk of losing your capital.

Q: How does the investment process work?

A: Your investment is not final until the project has met its investment target. Until then, the money should be held securely in an independent escrow account at a US bank. If the minimum is not met, the escrow account will return 100 percent of your investment directly to you. If the investment is met, the money is transferred to an account generally controlled by an asset management team, which only releases it if the property owner or developer has met the guidelines set forth in the contract.

Q: Is real estate investing safer than investing in stocks? Is it a safe investment?

A: It's a safer investment, but not entirely safe. Historically, REEs do very well, consistently well, and that's what makes the biggest difference. But it is about balancing and diversifying your portfolio, and stocks have a place in that.

The REE may not be an expert on the stock market but he or she should be a credible authority in his or her particular real estate strategy or niche. In addition, the REE can guide you on which strategies offer greater rewards (with greater risk) or smaller rewards (with less risk).

Q: What kind of profits can I expect?

A: There is really no way to know, much less guarantee, what kind of profits you can expect. We submit each property to rigorous financial tests, trying to ascertain the most likely outcome of your investment. Our team has a pretty solid track record and maintains transparency as long as you are our partner.

If you get any guarantees or promises of ROI, run the other way! Having said that, the private placement memorandum (PPM) will outline the investment expectations which include expected cash on cash return and other returns on investment. You may have heard the phrase "always under promise and over perform." This is particularly true in investing. Keep this in mind when you are reviewing your PPM and discussing the investment with the REE.

Q: What kind of properties do you invest in?

A: Based on our research and our desired financial outcome, our niche or "sweet spot" is commercial multifamily properties of one hundred units or more. We look for assets that are stable, with solid cash-flow performance and modest upside potential, and are expected to appreciate over the following five to seven years.

Most REEs have a niche that they prefer to work in. This is usually based on the business goals. You should expect a well thought-out formulated answer. If the REE really has given this much thought, he or she will want to share this and the expert reasoning behind his or her decision.

Q: How are returns estimated for my real estate investment?

A: This will vary, depending on how the deal is structured. Each investment should be reviewed on an individual basis. Be wary of the REE that tells you "we guarantee returns of XX percent" A great deal of scrutiny of the facts is required before coming up with the prospective return estimates. You will usually receive this information in your offering memorandum or commitment letter (in the case of smaller projects requiring fewer investors) provided by the REE.

Chapter 3:

What Kind of Investor are You?

Traditional retirement planning goes something like this:

1. Start saving early by putting your money into a 401(k) or IRA.
2. Keep adding to your investment and reinvesting the profits until you reach the age of sixty-five.
3. Hope that your investments appreciate or grow over time.
4. Then, once you have built up your "nest egg" and are ready to retire, start selling off a certain percentage of your portfolio each year to pay your living expenses until it's completely gone (hopefully not before you die).

Don't run out of time.

Traditional retirement investment planning is just not cutting it for millions of "baby boomers" who are currently contemplating retirement. There are a couple big problems with this plan.

First, you need to have a crystal ball that tells you how long you will live and how much money you will need. What happens if your money runs out before you do?

Second, because of inflation and other factors, you may find out you didn't save enough to last once you get there and it's too late. That is, unless you make significant cuts in your lifestyle or go back to work.

Third, you had better hope that your investments appreciate and that the market doesn't crash right before retirement. We all know people who had planned on retiring in 2007 but had most of their portfolios destroyed almost overnight when the market crashed.

Last, and the biggest problem with this plan, is that retirees have to withdraw their retirement savings to cover living expenses at retirement, therefore depleting their "nest eggs." This can put them in a very scary place if they live longer than expected, or if costs go up. Also, wouldn't you like to have something left to pass on to your loved ones?

This is a scary and uncertain future that millions of baby boomers face when contemplating retirement. Unfortunately, this is what most people are told is "solid retirement planning." And, it works for only some of them.

Consider an alternative retirement investment path to your happy retirement. It is an alternative plan that allows you the same advantages of the traditional option, but with fewer of the disadvantages. Think about this: what if you could put at least some of your retirement savings into an investment vehicle that would not only grow your investment over time, but also provide income that you could live off during retirement without having to deplete your investment?

This alternative type of retirement plan can be achieved through investment real estate. So, now you are thinking, "Didn't the housing market crash, too?" and "I don't want to deal with tenants." That is where you need to be careful. Like stocks or bonds, there are many different types of real estate and real estate investments that you can take part in. We will discuss a few in this book. There are high-risk and low-risk real estate deals. There are opportunities that require you to manage them yourself and take tenant calls and fix toilets. Most people only know about these types of opportunities. You can take part in these, but if you are getting ready to retire, that is probably the last thing you are interested in.

What most soon-to-be retirees don't know about are *private equity investments*. These opportunities are commonly not advertised, and you have to find out about them from someone who is putting them together, which is why most people don't know about them. They can give you all of the same benefits of real estate investing (monthly income, shielding your income from taxes, and appreciation), but you as a private money partner—as opposed to being the entrepreneur—do not have to take care of any of the day-to-day operations, calls from tenants, or leaky toilets. Normally, the sponsor or managing member of the private equity investment takes care of all of those operations for you, so the experience for you is just like any other investment where you receive your reports on how the investment is doing, but without a lot of the volatility of the more fluid equity markets.

These alternative investments can be excellent for retirees or people investing for retirement. They can provide a return on your investment, can provide for tax shelters, and can also appreciate in value. They are less volatile to global events than stocks are, and you don't have to sell off your equity to receive income from them. This can give you something to pass on to your children and grandchildren someday.

Now, we would never suggest putting all of your "eggs" in any one basket. Meeting with professionals is essential for planning out your retirement, as everyone's goals and needs are different. However, private equity investments in real estate are a great option, and something that we recommend everyone consider for part of their retirement portfolio.

So, what kind of investor are you?

At the risk of stating the obvious—If you are expecting to be a private money partner, you need to have some money.

Generally, the minimum expected investment may be as little as $5,000. But accredited investors may invest far more, depending upon the property, organization, exit strategy, and risk tolerance.

According to the Securities and Exchange Commission (SEC):

The Accredited Investor—Not only have you been investing for quite some time (not necessarily in real estate products), but you have at least $1,000,000 in assets (not including your primary residence) or you earn at least $200,000 a year, or have a combined household income of at least $300,000. This may sound familiar, but it bears repeating.

The Sophisticated Investor—You don't have the kind of wealth an accredited investor may have, but you know a bit more about the real estate side of things. This makes you "sophisticated" in your knowledge of real estate investing. Still, you may not be qualified (according to the SEC) to invest in certain real estate deals. You will want to discuss the details with the REE that you are working with.

You may have a retirement portfolio you want to diversify. Whether that portfolio is in a 401(k), an IRA, or life insurance, you may qualify as either an accredited or sophisticated investor just based on your retirement nest egg. But even if you don't, there are still ways that you can partner with a REE.

Lets talk a little about using your 401(k), IRA, or whole life policy.

You may use the actual funds, or in some cases you can borrow against these funds.

It's important, however, that you talk to your accountant or financial advisor about what you expect to do. However, when you speak to your investment advisor, don't be surprised if he or she tries to convince you that it's a bad idea. Remember, it's in your investment advisor's best interest that you keep your funds with him or her. Please be aware of your advisor's motivation.

So, first consider the IRA and 401(k). You may have either or both, and you, like most people, probably have the traditional or Roth. Because real estate investments are not a part of the IRA and 401(k) investing portfolio of accepted investments you cannot use your traditional or Roth IRA or 401(k) to invest in real estate. If you take the money out before retirement, you have to pay taxes on the amount you took out, plus a penalty. And, although you can borrow up to 50 percent of your 401(k) funds, you do have to pay them back with interest. The best alternative is to roll your traditional IRA and 401(k) funds over in to a self-directing IRA or self-directed 401(k).

Once you have a self-directed IRA or self-directed 401(k) you can use that money to invest in real estate. And the best way to do this is to be a private investor. In a nutshell...you lend the money (in a debt partnership) so that the REE can invest it into a property where interest and profits from that investment will be returned to the SD-IRA or SD 401(k). And when you consider what you've been earning with that money, it is, in my opinion, a no-brainer. If you are considering a SD-IRA or SD-401(k) it's important to get the right information before making your decision. The REE you work with should be able to help you find the right financial company to help you make the transition. Three of the best are

- Broad Financial
- Equity Trust
- The Entrust Group

All three have exceptionally helpful information about both self-directed IRAs and self-directed 401(k)s on their websites.

Self-directed IRAs and 401(k)s give you the power to invest your retirement savings into investments that you know and understand, and achieve returns in excess of traditional IRA or 401(k) options.

Let's touch briefly on the whole life policy. Not all whole life policies are created equal. What we're talking about is the concept of *infinite banking*. It's not new, although the term may sound foreign. In a sense you are your own bank—you are banking on yourself. To learn more about this we recommend you go to www.Paradigmlife.net/infinite-banking. This is also called perpetual financing. Just Google these terms and you will find information on this. This may or may not be right for you.

Frequently Asked Questions (These are questions you should ask yourself, as well as questions you should ask a real estate entrepreneur.)

Q: Why should I invest with a real estate entrepreneur when I could do this on my own (and probably make more money)?

A: Go for it! Just remember this—like any business owner, a REE should be well educated in his or her business, have a strong, experienced team, and be devoted to creating the best experience for his or her clients. This takes time—lots of it. As an investor you want your money to do the work for you, and it is a REE's business to make that happen.

Q: What is my risk tolerance? How much money can I afford to have tied up (with no access), and for how long?

A: Risk is inevitable. Unless you put your money under a mattress (and even then there is the risk of theft) you will have risk. Your major concern should be, "If I take this money and invest in real estate for X amount of time, will I be certain I won't need it for something else?" Good REEs will help you consider these things. They will ask you some tough questions and may even tell you that you can't invest with them. Listen to them. Don't just go to someone else who will take your money; you may regret it.

Q: Do I need the money I'm investing to live on? or could I live on the money this investment will make me?

A: So, you want your money to do the work. Consider the size of your nut and how much it would earn you to live on. Let's imagine you have $700,000 in an IRA. You are currently making 4 percent (average) on this money after considering inflation. Consider what would happen if you took half of this money and invested in stabilized, cash-flowing real estate that earns you 10 percent (average after inflation). How would that affect the way you live? Consider the alternative: taking half that money and putting it into a high-risk stock fund! (Need we say more?) *No one is suggesting the real estate investing is without risk.*

Q: So, we talked about risk. Doesn't the real estate entrepreneur have an effect on risk?

A: Simply put, yes. It's extremely important for you to interview the REE and ask questions. As with any investing, certain strategies will attract certain types of investors. Riskier investments generally mean higher returns, but can also mean bigger and faster losses. Remember the real estate collapse? Who lost the most? The speculators. Who came out of it virtually unscathed? The cash-flow investors. How the REE evaluates a property and structures the deals can have an effect on risk. The type of exit strategy can have an effect on risk. When the REE invests in the market cycle can have an effect on risk.

Q: Do I pass the accredited investor test? or am I a sophisticated investor?

A: As described in a previous chapter, you must earn at least $200,000 as an individual, $300,000 as a couple, or have a net worth of at least $1.0 million, not including your primary residence. If you don't qualify, you may be considered a sophisticated investor.

Some REEs will only work with accredited investors because of the types of deals they do. As a sophisticated investor you may find you are only able to invest in smaller deals. Remember, as you "work your way up" you will become an accredited investor.

Q: Can I lose my money?

A: As with any investment, there is risk. But as we have already covered, compared to stocks your risk may be minimal. That is based on the type of exit strategy your REE offers. You should always know what the exit strategy is. Inherently the least risky is the multifamily cash flow strategy—slow, steady income, and not a lot of volatility. Next is the multifamily cash flow (emerging market) strategy, providing slow steady income with potentially larger profits at sale of the property in five to seven years. Flips (commercial or single-family) carry greater rewards, much faster and bigger profits, but a higher risk of loss. Bottom line— Yes, as with any investment, there is the risk of losing your money.

Q: What is a self-directed IRA?

A: Self-directed IRAs are nearly the same as normal IRAs. The only difference is that you are able to choose where your money is invested from all of the available investment options (stocks, bonds, real estate, businesses, or even apartment complexes) instead of being limited to traditional IRA investments such as stocks, bonds, and mutual funds. This is very attractive, especially for those who have investment experience and who know how to manage their funds in order to obtain maximum profits while still enjoying all the benefits of traditional IRAs (tax deductions, tax-free profits, and estate planning).

Q: What are the benefits of a self-directed IRA or self-directed 401(k)?

A: Taxes: Self-directed IRAs and 401(k)s allow taxes on assets held inside the IRA or 401(k) account to be deferred or postponed until the money is withdrawn from the account at retirement. With alternative investments, account owners can take a proactive approach toward improving investment returns because they can choose assets that are not publicly marketed. Additionally, if invested in real estate, taxes on appreciation and rental income are deferred, so an investor can grow his or her portfolio at an even faster rate.

Diversification: Account holders can make both traditional and alternative investments within self-directed IRAs and 401(k)s. The self-directed IRA and 401(k) allows people to diversify into many different assets.

Control: With self-directed IRAs and 401(k)s, you will be able to take control of your retirement savings and place your money in investments that you understand. You aren't stuck waiting for the ups and downs of the stock market to determine your return. Multiple streams of income are possible. When investing in real estate, you can benefit from appreciation of your asset, cash flow generated, and loan principal pay-down by your tenants.

Q: What can I invest in with a self-directed IRA, and what is not allowed?

A: Self-directed IRAs are specialized accounts that allow their holders to invest in anything except for life insurance, collectibles, and investments that would personally benefit them or close family members, as restricted by the IRS. Real estate, private placements, and businesses, among other things, are common investments within self-directed IRAs. Be sure to talk to a knowledgeable self-directed IRA advisor to find out if your desired investment is qualified.

See chapter 6, "Legal Issues with Real Estate Investments," for additional information on self-directed IRAs.

Chapter 4:

The Real Estate Market (Cycle)—How Do Real Estate Entrepreneurs Read the Market?

As a private money partner, it is important that you have a fundamental understanding of the real estate market cycle and how REEs use it to make investments that will create what they desire in the way of risk and profit.

You may or may not have heard the phrase "make your money when you buy." In real estate terms that means that you shouldn't speculate on what might happen to your property, but look at what is happening right now. A savvy real estate entrepreneur studies each market he or she enters. It's kind of the same way a fisherman looks at a river. Most of us see the river, how fast the current might be, and a picturesque landscape. Seasoned fishermen see something quite different. They read the river, notice the currents and eddies, and see the shadows and the rocks where fish might be. At a glance they know exactly where to drop their line and, with a bit of patience, hook the big ones.

It's much the same in real estate. Most people have a vague sense of how their own town is doing, or even how the country is doing as a whole. They may have a good idea about what's happening around the country because they listen to the media and the Yahoo! reports, but they really have no idea what the market is doing in any specific part of the country. When a professional reads a real estate market, he or she sees something very different. REEs can tell you the specifics about construction, job growth, revitalization or enterprise zones, the path of progress, and a host of other indicators that tell them where they should or should not buy, or to wait a little longer, or that the time to buy has passed.

This leads us in to the real estate market cycle and its four primary phases. Where the market is within that cycle dictates how the REE invests in his or her properties. So, what do real estate entrepreneurs look for? Why is knowing the cycle so important?

The simple answer is that knowing how each stage works and how it affects the strategy will make money for both the REEs and their private investors. But in addition to that, REEs who know how to use the market cycle in the location they have chosen to invest to their advantage will make the most money in each stage of the cycle.

There are two buyer phases and two seller phases. It is the combination of ten main criteria and the characteristics presented in each one of these criteria that the savvy REE studies to determine what part of the cycle any given market is in—and more importantly, how that determines his or her investing strategy.

Every type of property follows these four phases, whether it is single-family homes, commercial/retail properties, or apartments—it's just that they are in these phases during different periods. For instance, apartment investments will experience strength before retail does. That's because renters can move into apartments very quickly after, say, a new factory opens in town. Retail will start to notice the stronger consumer demand and then build to take advantage of it. It's cause and effect. The last to see the increase in demand is single-family housing, which happens once families begin to settle into an area when jobs are secure and long-term residency is evident.

How long does it take for a market to complete all phases in the cycle? Full rotation can take anywhere from ten to twenty-five years. Cities on the East and West Coasts tend to change more rapidly from phase to phase than the cities in the heartland. Obviously there is a big gap between ten and twenty-five years, and this is where understanding the signs and signals aid the REE in determining whether the cycle is closer to ten years, fifteen years, or twenty-five years.

To give you a better idea of what goes into this, let's look at a few of the criteria and what happens during each of the four phases. Once a knowledgeable REE has studied the characteristics of each phase of a market cycle, he or she can very quickly and expertly look at any real estate market and know what phase it is in, and use that information to determine where to invest based on the exit strategy.

Following is a simplified version of the indicators of each market phase. This information has been included in the guide so that you have a better understanding of the research that goes into finding profitable properties. A savvy REE should have a solid understanding of this market cycle and how it affects an investing strategy.

Buyer's Market Phase I:

The market is oversupplied with commercial properties. Supply is one of the key market forces that cause a market to go from boom to bust and back again.

Think of a real estate market as a large cruise ship out on the ocean. The captain can decide to change direction in an instant, but the ship takes a long time to respond to the captain's orders. If the captain becomes impatient and orders another course change before the ship has responded to the first, he or she has overcorrected.

This also happens in real estate. Inexperienced real estate entrepreneurs will make snap judgments based on what they see happening in the market right now, but forget to consider the time it takes to set investments such as new construction and development in motion. This sparks more demand, creates more supply, and soon, just as with the cruise ship, things are headed in the wrong direction and there is a glut on the market. Price cutting takes hold.

To make matters worse, Buyer's Market Phase 1 typically coincides with stagnant or negative job growth in the area. The market will reach a point at which unemployment peaks and investment property values will decline to their lowest levels of any phase in the cycle.

Confident REEs will resist the urge to buy into every good-looking deal, but they know that good cash flow is worth the investment. This is the best time to apply the flip strategy. Profits should be kept in cash until Buyer's Market Phase II. A confident investor also uses this stage to look for exceptional deals.

Buyer's Market Phase II:

To facilitate the movement of Buyer's Market Phase I to Buyer's Market Phase II, a few things must happen. The local leadership must do something to increase employment opportunities. As jobs are created, people begin to migrate back into a community. The population begins to increase and vacancies begin to fill—and once the occupancy rate rises to a healthy level, rents go up. Communities *must* take a proactive approach; this doesn't happen on its own. A master plan is created and implemented—the key word being "implemented." REEs are attracted and this sparks new growth.

As the market continues to improve, properties morph from being occupied by anyone who can pay a few dollars in rent to fulfilling their highest and best use. They attract higher income residents and rents continue to increase. In Buyer's Market Phase I, rents were at their lowest levels, but now they're on the move...up. Because of this, property values also rise. This is where the emerging market begins, and it is the sweet spot for many real estate entrepreneurs.

Seller's Market, Phase I

As the market begins to reach equilibrium, rental and lease rates have risen to the level that can support new construction of commercial properties. As the emerging market continues, investors now see positive signs everywhere they look, and demand for investment properties is at its highest point of any phase in the cycle. Demand begins to surpass supply, and construction continues at a feverish pace. The moment a property comes on the market, there is a bidding war and sales prices often exceed asking prices. This is a *hot* market....sellers are in nirvana! Buyers see the value because rents are up and life is good. The market has emerged as we enter the next phase.

Seller's Market, Phase II

This is the riskiest phase of the market cycle. As the frenzy begins to ease up—because the market begins to saturate—properties begin to stay on the market longer. With the days of multiple offers gone, office and retail space is getting filled up, but not snatched up. Sellers are still getting top dollar for their properties, and rents are still high, but sales and leases just aren't happening as fast. For the first time since the Buyer's Market Phase II began, business and job growth begin to slow.

The most important take-away for you as the private money partner is to understand that the market cycle can be in any one of these phases at any given time in various locations around the country. Where Richmond, Virginia, may be in Seller's Market Phase I, Louisville, Kentucky, may be in Buyer's Market Phase II and Las Vegas, Nevada, may be in Buyer's Market Phase I, and so on. Although it's rare to see all market phases happening at one time throughout the country, it is very common to see different metropolitan areas at various stages throughout the same phase in the cycle.

The Emerging Market

So, what's the big deal about the emerging market? You may feel, based on what you have just read, that the best time to invest in real estate is during an "emerging market," but what does that really mean? First, remembering the market cycle, an emerging market for single family happens at a different time than an emerging market for multifamily, which happens at a different time than an emerging market for retail and office, and so on. In addition to considering the type of real estate, the REE also must consider the desired outcome and thus the exit strategy of the investment asset. It is true that if you are looking for increased cash-flow opportunity and the potential for higher profits at sale, then looking for property in an emerging market may be a bit more lucrative.

How the Market Cycle Affects Investing

REEs need to consider the market cycle and each of its phases if they are to get the best results on their investments. They will want to consider the exit strategy—as in a buy-fix-sell versus a buy and hold property when looking at the phases. They must be flexible. Knowing at what point to stop flipping and start holding is vital and can mean the difference in making thousands or losing thousands. No matter how much REEs know about properties and exit strategies, it's knowing how to assess the market cycle and use it to their advantage that will make or break their business.

As a general rule, the real estate entrepreneur knows that the best time to buy depends on the *exit* strategy.

Frequently Asked Questions

Q: Why does it matter whether the REE understands the market cycle?

A: First, REEs don't need to know the market cycle of, say, Albuquerque, New Mexico, if they are investing in Louisville, Kentucky, but they should know the Louisville market like the proverbial "back of their hand." They should have full knowledge of where in the cycle their chosen real estate market is. They should be able to tell you why they prefer residential to commercial based on what the local market is doing. If they don't understand or follow the market cycle, they could end up like all of those REEs who lost their shirts and—more importantly—lost all of their investors' money in the last real estate collapse.

Q: How does the cycle affect my bottom line, or my return on investment (ROI)?

A: If a property is held for too long or not long enough, that can seriously affect your ROI. If your REE is inflexible and buys only multifamily, he or she needs to consider when to buy and when not to buy because it may be a better market for retail or industrial properties. It's not the cycle itself that has the impact on your ROI, but it's when the savvy REE buys and sells and the types of properties and exit strategies the REE employs.

Q: Is there a wrong time to buy?

A: There is never really a wrong time to buy. It just depends on what the exit strategy is versus the phase in the market cycle at the local market level.

Q: How does the market cycle affect the exit strategy?

A: Consider the market cycle as a gauge. Each phase impacts the timing of a purchase or sale. If a REE wants to buy a property to flip in four to six months, he or she will want to be sure to get the most value out of that sale. Knowing where the local market is in its cycle will help the REE determine if it's better to flip, rehab, and hold for a short term or perhaps forgo residential altogether and consider multifamily, retail, or commercial.

Q: I work with a REE who just buys for cash flow. Should I be concerned about the cycle?

A: You should have an understanding of the cycle. This will help you understand what the REE is doing. If you're concerned, ask questions. Never just follow the REE blindly. That's the purpose of this book—to open your eyes!

Q: How does the real estate market cycle relate to the stock market cycle?

A: You have seen in this latest (and by no means last) housing collapse. Both are tied to the economy, the banks, and the government...and don't forget the perceptions—positive and negative—as well as the fears of the population.

Chapter 5:

Which Types of Properties Should You Invest In?

One of the things you should consider as a **private money partner** is in what kind of properties you want to invest. Knowing this will help you focus on the return on investment possibilities available. In addition to the effect of the exit strategy on the ROI, the property type can be a critical segment of the equation.

When considering an investment, you need to ask yourself whether the properties are, for example, single-family properties, multifamily properties, or commercial properties (including office, retail and industrial). Each type of real estate has a different set of drivers influencing its performance; each investment provides its own unique income possibility. That means when you make an investment, it is important to consider the characteristics of the real estate, because the performance of those properties will impact the performance of your investment.

So which type of property should you invest in?

Single Family

Investing in single-family residential properties can be a lucrative investment in any economy, as long as there is a sound strategy for investing. Single-family properties can be purchased as distressed homes, foreclosures, fixer-uppers, or in ready-to-use condition. Single-family residential means a structure maintained and used as a single dwelling unit. The single-family residential (SFR) is typically defined in many zoning codes as a single dwelling unit (a single household) per parcel. The building does not share an inside wall with any other house or dwelling. It has only outside walls and does not touch any other dwelling. In the world of the REE, "single family" will also refer to duplex, fourplex, or any property under five units—at which point it becomes a commercial multifamily property (based on lending rules).

Some real estate entrepreneurs ignore these types of investment properties because they don't understand how single-family properties can equal big profits. They get caught up in the "go big" mentality and miss out on some of the most profitable investments that can be found just down the street. Contrary to what some REEs believe, you don't have to buy multifamily properties to make a big profit. The REE who is willing to work hard can provide investors with big profits. Smaller properties can provide investment opportunities if the REE knows how best to utilize these investment properties.

Multifamily Residential

Multifamily real estate is a type of residential housing in which there is more than one residence within one building or complex. The most common form of multifamily real estate is apartment buildings. We define smaller multifamily properties as those having five to one hundred apartments or units. This size of property can be a great fit for individual or a small group of investors. At this size, the income can adequately cover the expenses of the property. Multifamily can also include student housing, rooming houses, and group homes.

You will find stable returns in multifamily residential property, because no matter what the economic cycle, people always need a place to live. The result is that in normal markets, and throughout most of the real estate market cycle (as discussed in chapter 4) residential occupancy tends to stay reasonably high. Another factor of this type of residential property is that the loss of a single tenant has a minimal impact on the bottom line, whereas if you lose a tenant in a single-family property the negative effects can be much more significant. Additional attributes that may favor multifamily investments include lower expense-to-income costs (commonly referred to as the expense ratio) as well as lower capital improvement costs (one roof for sixteen units versus one roof for one house).

In multifamily property you may hear the term *class*...as in Class A, Class B, C, or D. This refers to the age and condition of the property and provides insight as to the expense ratio and subsequently the value of the property. Generally, the older the building, the higher the expense ratio, which subsequently affects the cash flow and the ROI. As risk goes, Class A (the newest properties) are the lowest risk, with Class D (otherwise known as "war zone") properties having the greatest risk.

Commercial

Commercial real estate is different from residential real estate in many ways. Commercial real estate involves companies, rather than individuals, as tenants. The deals are much bigger, so the profits can also be very lucrative. However, with the potential for large profit comes greater risk.

Commercial real estate can be very rewarding, but you should not go into investing without understanding the risks involved. The term "commercial property" includes parcels, with or without buildings, used for business or retail purposes. Investments in commercial real estate involve a significant cash commitment and you will likely find yourself part of a bigger investment group to purchase larger commercial properties.

Office

Offices are preferred properties for many real estate entrepreneurs. They tend to be, on average, the largest and highest profile property type. They are typically found in downtown and sprawling suburban office parks. Returns from office properties can be highly variable because the market tends to be sensitive to economic performance. One downside is that office buildings have high operating costs, so if you lose a tenant it can have an impact on the returns for the property. However, in times of prosperity, offices tend to perform well, because demand for space causes rental rates to increase significantly.

Industrial

Industrial property is often considered the "staple" of the average REE. Generally, they require smaller average investments, are less management intensive, and have lower operating costs than office and retail properties. There are varying types of industrial properties, depending on the use of the building. For example, buildings could be used for storage, warehousing, manufacturing, research and development, or distribution.

All Those Choices!

A problem that troubles several would-be private investors is the quantity of choices available. A very logical and rational explanation to this dilemma may help you make an intelligent choice. There are many types of real estate to invest in, and just as many ways and reasons to invest.

One of the key differences between investing in a piece of real estate as compared to stocks or bonds is that real estate is an investment in the building and the land it is built upon. This makes real estate highly tangible, because unlike most stocks you can see and touch your property.

From single-family rentals to large multifamily properties to commercial high-rises and industrial property, investing in real estate brings rewards to many. The key to making good investment decisions in real estate lies in research. Investing of all kinds can be precarious, but can also be very rewarding if done properly. The key to successful investing is to fully understand the workings of investments and to seek advice from experienced REEs whom you are considering investing with. Of all other possible investments that are within the reach of the average investor, none offer the combination of outstanding benefits that are available to private real estate investors.

To Flip or To Hold?

Different real estate investments have their own advantages and disadvantages. The opportunities that exist in real estate, compared to average returns on other investments, explain its popularity.

A term made popular by several television shows is *flipping*. You will also hear the terms *rehabbing, fix-and-flip,* or *buy-fix-sell.* The concept is that a property in need of repair is purchased below market value to fix up and sell as quickly as possible. This can be done with a single-family, multifamily (often referred to as "repositioning"), or any type of commercial property. Although real estate is an investment that doesn't convert readily to cash, single-family properties are generally considered to be the most liquid of all real property investments. They typically can be sold in a shorter period of time than other types of real estate. Flipping single-family properties is the most common form of real estate strategy, but, in our opinion, is a real estate job for the REE and one that requires a lot of hard work and long hours. The hold or cashflow strategy, is the preferred method for building long-term wealth.

When many people think of a real estate investing, they picture a single home. A single-family property is also an easily rentable type of investment real estate, since everyone certainly needs housing. For decades, investors have built fortunes from owning single-family properties. When purchased correctly, single-family properties can be a great way to build wealth and a cash-flowing real estate portfolio. However, as many REEs have found, investing in multifamily and commercial real estate can be an even better way to bring in cash. Cash flow is important in any investment, and in almost every case, the multifamily property brings significantly higher cash flow than the single-family property. Although many REEs will have a particular investment niche, to be heavily weighted in just one category is never an advantage. As a private investor you should consider multiple strategies for your investments for the same reason you would diversify a stock portfolio.

Building Wealth

There is no question that fortunes have been made in real estate. From **Robert Kiyosaki** and **Donald Trump** to, perhaps, your-brother-in-law, people have made money investing in real estate. They invest in real estate because of its tremendous advantages over other forms of investments.

They can make money when they buy.
They can make money when they own.
They can make money when they sell.

As a **private money partner**, you can be a part of this.

Chapter 6:

Legal Issues with Real Estate Investments

This chapter was written by our business attorney, David Stoyanoff (see his bio at the end of the chapter). David has helped us form LLCs, trusts, and venture partnerships, and has prepared other documents when we are partnering with private investors. His goal here is to help you understand what the real estate entrepreneur (which he refers to simply as investor) must consider as part of any real estate partnership or transaction.

The reason I felt it was necessary to include this chapter was to help you as you meet with real estate entrepreneurs to ask questions about how they form the business entities, partnerships, trusts, and so forth. As a partner, you are subject to all of the legal issues with real estate investment.

All businesses should have a business attorney on their team. This is especially true for real estate entrepreneurs, who may form multiple partnerships throughout their careers.   *Anca Markie*

Successful real estate investors prefer to concentrate their efforts on profitable acquisitions and positive cash flow operations. It is also important, however, to protect against liabilities. Even though real estate investment is generally a "passive" activity, accidents and injuries raise the issue of liability. Owners of real estate investments can protect their assets from these potential claims by having adequate insurance in place and by forming a legal entity to hold title to the property and separate the investor from the liabilities of the property.

Types of Legal Entities

- Corporation

- LLC

- Partnership

- Business Trust ("Series Entity")

- Sole Proprietorship (not a real legal entity)

An investor has several options for the structure of the legal entity that holds the real estate, including **limited liability companies, corporations,** and **business trusts**. A limited liability company ("LLC") gives liability protection and is easy to form and maintain. A corporation provides liability protection like an LLC. In either case, if an injury occurs, the victim's recourse is against the entity, rather than the investor.

Corporations are the historical entity used by businesses to protect owners from the claims of business creditors. The corporation dates back to English common law and the joint stock company. These were formed as a means to raise capital to explore new lands and exploit the resources found there. (Essentially, the first real estate deals in America were done by corporations.) Today, a US corporation requires much the same formalities as were required five hundred years ago. These include three levels of management (shareholders, directors, and officers), stock certificates, and periodic meetings of stockholders to elect directors, and meetings of directors to manage the company.

Limited Liability Companies offer a number of advantages over other entities for real estate investors.

Liability protection is the key advantage of both corporations and LLCs over partnerships or sole proprietorships. Virginia is one of thirteen states that protects the assets inside an LLC from a charging order. Judgment creditors of an owner (**"Member"**) are only entitled to the member's distributions. Creditors of the members cannot foreclose on the LLC's property. This protects the real estate held by the LLC and the members from the bad acts of their comembers.

Flexibility—As compared with corporations, an LLC can be much more flexible. The modern LLC began thirty-five years ago with the Wyoming Limited Liability Act. The original LLC was structured like a partnership, but without unlimited liability that partners face. As a child of partnership law, the LLC statutes give great deference to the LLC operating agreement. If the LLC members do the following three things, they can do just about anything they want with the LLC:

1. Write down the rules of allocating rights, duties, profits, losses, voting, and liquidation rights.

2. Ensure the results do not defraud the creditors or investors and are consistent with public policy.

3. Ensure the tax results have substantial economic effect.

Multiple LLCs

Many investors choose to own their real estate investments in an LLC. However, if the investor owns multiple properties, liability protection can be more complicated.

> **Example:** An investor owns three rental properties and transfers them all to his newly formed LLC with himself as the single member. One of his tenant's guests is injured at property A, wins a lawsuit, and obtains a judgment against the LLC. The guest records his judgment as liens against properties A, B, and

C. Under this scenario, until the investor clears the liens, he cannot sell property B or C and give clear title to the buyer.

One solution to the problem in the example is to form separate, individual LLCs to hold each property. However, this solution can get expensive and unwieldy when investors own more than three or four properties. A common compromise is to hold no more than three properties in each LLC. While this does protect some of the investor's real estate and assets, the other two properties in the LLC are still potentially at risk.

History of Business Trusts

A business trust is an unincorporated business organization created by a legal document, a declaration of trust, and used in place of a corporation or partnership for the transaction of various kinds of business with limited liability.

Massachusetts allowed the first business trusts in the early 1900s largely because corporations could not own real estate at that time. Delaware enacted a business trust law in 1988. Twenty-nine states now have business trust statutes. For example, Nevada allows series to be formed within a Nevada LLC.

"Series entities" like the Virginia Business Trust are becoming more popular, and have been authorized by several states. Many mutual funds operate as business trusts, as do many real estate investment trusts (REITs).

Forming and Maintaining a Business Trust

To form a Virginia business trust, articles of trust are filed with the SCC and a "governing instrument" (the contract that controls the trust) is drafted, as required by law. The trust is governed by trustees who are similar to the board of directors of a corporation. The owners of a business trust are called *beneficial owners*, and are like shareholders.

The governing instrument can create a separate series for each piece of real estate owned by the trust. This provides liability protection between each piece of property owned by the business trust.

The business trust must keep records of minutes of meetings of owners and all correspondence with owners. Also, under the statute, *it is essential to keep separate financial books and records for each series*. The governing instrument must specifically authorize the formation of separate series.

Like an LLC, a business trust can elect its tax treatment. A trust with a single owner can be taxed like any other real estate investment, and reported on the owner's individual Form 1040. If there are multiple owners, the trust will likely be taxed as a partnership. In either case, there is no requirement that each individual series be reported separately on the owners' tax return(s)—but again, don't forget the state law requirement to keep separate books and records for each series.

The Importance of Formalities

By state statutes an entity *must* do certain things. Failure to do these things may wipe out the liability protection the entity provides. This is often described as *"piercing the corporate veil."*

Corporations require annual meetings, annual reports, bylaws, and stock certificates. These are statutory requirements. It is important to keep these annual minutes and organizational documents up-to-date. Most corporations have a minute book to hold these original documents, usually kept by the corporation's attorney or registered agent.

On the other hand, the LLC operating agreement is the contract that governs the entity along with articles of organization. It is much easier to maintain LLC documents because they have fewer requirements in the statutes. Although some LLCs are organized like corporations, requiring boards of managers, annual member meetings, and membership certificates, none of these are required by the Virginia statute. All you really need is a written operating agreement. If the LLC enters into a transaction, you will likely need a written *resolution* to show that the members have agreed to it.

Other key steps to help ensure your legal entity is respected:

- Sign in the name of the entity. Use the complete and exact entity name, including "LLC" or "Inc."

- Officers should use their titles when signing ("President," "Managing Member").

- Keep separate bank accounts for each entity.

- Keep separate books and records for each entity and each business trust *series.*

- Have written documents for every transaction.

- Keep transactions between the entity and its owners at *arms' length*—that is, with terms that you would find in similar transactions between unrelated parties.

Land Trusts

A *land trust* is a traditional trust, not a separate legal entity. As a trust, it has three parties involved: the *grantor* or *trustor* who creates the trust and contributes money or property to it, the *trustee* who holds title to the assets in the trust, and the *beneficial owner* or *beneficiary*, who enjoys the benefit of the trust income and assets, as provided for in the trust document. A beneficiary's interest in the trust is called *beneficial interest*. In any trust there can be more than one of each of these parties.

Though not a legal entity, a land trust can protect the beneficial owner of the property in several ways:

- Privacy—The trustee holds legal title on the deed. The beneficiary's name can be disclosed only by court order.
- Beneficial interest is personal property—Creditors of beneficiary cannot place liens on the property, but can reach beneficial interest if known.
- Beneficial interests can be transferred easily.

Land Trust Basics

The creation of a land trust starts with the trust agreement between trustee and beneficiary. Under the agreement, the trustee holds legal title to a piece of real estate. The deed to the land trust names the trustee and the trust (e.g., "Joe Investor, Trustee, 123 Main Street Land Trust").

The beneficiary has the power to direct the trustee regarding the property management, sale, lease, and operation under the terms of the trust agreement. Under the trust agreement, the beneficiary holds a beneficial interest in the trust. This interest is personal property held by the beneficiary, not real property (fixed property, principally land and buildings).

Opportunities

- The beneficiary has the tax advantages of property ownership, since they have all rights to control the property.
- Beneficiaries can acquire properties anonymously.

- Legal entities can be a trustee or beneficiary to further shield investors from liability.
- May be used creatively to create cotenants or partnerships, or to subdivide properties.

Tax Issues with Real Estate Investments

Taxation of Business Entities

C corporations pay double tax: a corporation's profits are taxed once at the corporate level and again when dividends are received by shareholders. This is commonly known as *double taxation*.

This double level of tax can be a serious problem when appreciated assets are distributed. The built-in gain is generally taxable at the corporate level upon distribution of appreciated property. Then, the distribution is taxed to the shareholder at fair market value.

> **Example:** Corporation owns a parcel of real estate which cost $100,000 but has a fair market value of $400,000. If that property is distributed to Shareholder, Corporation pays tax on the built-in gain ($400,000 − $100,000 = $300,000) and Shareholder pays tax on the fair market value of the distributed property ($400,000).

On the other hand, partnerships, LLCs, and S corporations are *flow-through* entities, which means the owners pay the income taxes.

Partnership taxation is usually recommended for most real estate holdings due to the flow-through of tax benefits and the high degree of flexibility in making special allocations. So with multiple investors, the typical structure is an LLC or a business trust, taxed as a partnership.

LLCs and business trusts are "disregarded entities" for tax purposes. With multiple owners they are taxed as partnerships, but may elect to be taxed as C or S corporations. However, partnership taxation is usually recommend for most real estate holdings. A single-member LLC is disregarded for tax purposes (taxed on owner's Form 1040). But again, even a single-member LLC can elect to be taxed as a C or S corporation.

A business trust with multiple owners can be taxed a partnership, but this is not 100 percent clear in all cases. If there is only one owner or the owners are a married couple, no separate tax return is required for the entity. Income and deductions are reported on the individuals' Form 1040 Schedule C or E, like an LLC.

S corporations have limited flexibility in making special allocations of profits, losses, and liquidation payments, because they are restricted to a single class of stock. There is also a restriction on the number of shareholders, and S corporations cannot have foreign shareholders.

With proper planning, S corporation shareholders do not pay self-employment taxes on profits.

Taxation of Entities Holding Real Estate

Tax treatment can depend on the level and type of activity. In general, income of real estate investors is considered passive:

- Gains are capital gains.
- Operating losses generally are not deductible against other income.
- There are no Social Security taxes on net investment income.

Dealers (or *flippers*) are typically treated as real estate professionals and their business is taxed as an active trade or business.

- Gains are taxed as ordinary income, not capital gains
- Operating losses can be used offset income from other sources

- Social Security taxes apply on all net income of the business

These are very general descriptions, and this is a complex area of the tax law. The tax treatment of an individual investor will depend on his or her individual facts and circumstances.

Risks of Personal Liability

There are certain acts or omissions that can impose personal liability on owners. One of the most important of these relates to the filing of all *tax returns* and the payment of all required taxes. This is particularly true with respect to employee withholding taxes. Taxes withheld from employee wages are held in trust on behalf of the employee and the government. The officer, shareholder, manager, or member can be *personally liable* if these funds are used for other company purposes.

Self-Directed IRAs

There are pros and cons of buying real estate within an IRA. Some investors use their IRA, not by withdrawing cash, but by having the IRA buy the property and hold it within the account. This is possible as long as it's not for a primary residence, assuming the IRA custodian is willing. Could it not be a feasible way to buy a potential future retirement property in a nice area? or to simply make an investment in, say, a bit of commercial property?

Dozens of investors asked pretty much the same thing. And the answer is yes, you can invest in real estate via a *self-directed* IRA.

The term "self-directed" is somewhat of a misnomer, in that you can't buy or manage an investment property directly. Rather, you have to go through a third-party IRA custodian. But otherwise, under Section 408 of the Internal Revenue Code, you can put your money to work in the residential or commercial real estate market.

You can even invest in raw land, property in foreign countries, real estate contracts, or the trust deeds that back up mortgages. And you can pool your resources with other investors.

One reason more people don't take advantage of this opportunity is that you must go beyond your bank or brokerage company to locate a custodian who specializes in real estate. Once you find the right person, you can "direct" him or her to invest your money in whatever you want on your behalf. But since the custodian you choose will hold title to the real estate, it's extremely important to select someone who specializes in the type of investment you want to make.

Rules for Self-Directed IRAs

IRS regulations prohibit you from using the property as your own residence or vacation home. You can't lease space from yourself in your IRA-held commercial property, either. And you can't place a property that you already own into your retirement account. Also precluded are investments in properties or secured loans that involve your son, daughter, parents, or other disqualified parties. You can't rent to them or buy properties from them that they already own.

Once you've chosen a property, *you cannot buy it in your name.* Your IRA custodian must actually purchase it in his or her name for your benefit. For example, the title might read "XYZ Co., custodian FBO (for the benefit of) John Doe IRA."

All income from the property must flow through to your IRA. It can't come directly to you. And all expenses, including taxes, insurance, and repairs, must be paid from funds in your account.

You can sell properties held in your IRA and use the proceeds to buy others, or you can simply hold your profits in your account. Another alternative is to sell your IRA-held property with seller financing so that all the payments for principal and interest are paid to your account.

After you reach retirement age, you can withdraw the real estate from the IRA and sell it yourself or use it as your residence or vacation home. If you are fifty-nine-and-a-half or older, the withdrawal is penalty-free, just like withdrawals from any other IRA. But you may have to pay income taxes.

This is when holding property in a Roth IRA offers several advantages. If the property has been held in a traditional IRA, you will have to pay taxes on the current value of the property at distribution. But if it was held in a Roth IRA, you won't. So if you expect to hold your investment for a long period and you anticipate that your real estate investments will appreciate over time, this may be an attractive option.

Final Thoughts

My practice is based in Virginia, so this chapter's focus is based on Virginia state law. State laws vary, so please consult local counsel before you make any key legal decisions.

David Stoyanoff provides advice and counsel to business clients primarily in the areas of entity selection and formation; commercial and private debt financing; real estate development and investment; and business sales, acquisitions, and reorganizations. He has worked extensively with business clients, devising multiple-entity corporate structures that provide asset protection and succession plans for business owners. Mr. Stoyanoff has over twenty-five years of business financial, legal, and tax experience. Prior to entering into the private practice of law in 2004, he held positions as assistant vice president of compensation and benefits, and senior tax counsel for CSX Corporation.
Mr. Stoyanoff was born in Sioux City, Iowa, and raised in Norfolk, Nebraska, where he completed high school. He graduated from Wayne State College and attended law school at the University of Nebraska, graduating in 1979. He was admitted to the Nebraska State Bar and the US District Court of Nebraska in 1979 and to the Virginia State Bar and US District Court of Virginia in 2004.

Mr. Stoyanoff is an active member of the Virginia State Bar and the American Bar Association. He is also a member of the Greater Richmond Chamber of Commerce, the Retail Merchants Association, and Business Network International (BNI).

www.toruslaw.com
david@TorusLaw.com

Frequently Asked Questions

Q: Who makes decisions in an LLC?

A: Decisions in an LLC are governed by a document called an *operating agreement*. While every operating agreement is slightly different, they usually include a managing member and limited members. The managing member typically makes all of the day-to-day decisions, and the limited members act as passive investors on the transaction. The managing member can determine how much cash to distribute to the limited members versus how much to hold in reserve, and assess possible sales for the property. There are certain activities that might mandate a vote by the limited members, and the limited members can typically take action if the managing member defaults on the terms of the agreement or is grossly negligent.

Q: If I invest with a real estate company or real estate entrepreneur and something happens to that company or entrepreneur, what will happen to my investment?

A: For equity investments, the REE operates LLCs that could be managed by a replacement manager. The REE or the REE's company would appoint an agent, such as a national bank or trust company, to manage the LLCs in the event the REE is unable to manage them.

For loan investments, the REE or the REE's company could be replaced by a loan servicing company. The REE would appoint such a company to manage the loan investments in the event he or she is unable to manage them.

Q: What are the tax implications of investing in real estate?

A: While we cannot provide legal or tax advice, and we recommend you speak with your own accountant or attorney, one of the benefits of investing in real estate equity through limited liability companies (LLCs) is that they can be taxed as partnerships, which allows for the entity to be "pass through." For example, profits, losses, and depreciation can be passed through to the investors, as applicable on equity investments.

Chapter 7:

The Debt Partnership

In private investing with a real estate entrepreneur, there are two kinds of investing partnerships. There is the equity investor or equity partner, and there is the debt investor or debt partner, which can also be commonly referred to as the private lender. Since the term *private lender* typically refers to the entrepreneurial endeavor of private lending, we prefer the term *debt partner* for private investor lending.

As a debt partner you lend your money to help the REE purchase the property. Your loan is secured by a mortgage note or trust deed held by you (if you are the only debt partner) or the LLC (if there are multiple debt partners). with the property as collateral. You have no additional interest in the property and therefore receive no profits from revenues.

The question you should ask yourself is "Which is best for me?" Before you can approach a REE you have to at least answer this first basic set of questions: "Do I prefer greater security with a lower rate of return?" or "Can I handle more risk for a greater reward?" This you must answer yourself. A good REE can help you consider the pros and cons of each option and help find that answer. During your "interview" process, the REE will discuss with you all aspects of your financial picture. If you don't feel comfortable sharing everything, that's OK. Just understand that if the REE doesn't have a clear picture, he or she can't give you a clear understanding of what may be best for you. So, to really understand this would be to first ask yourself, "What is my risk tolerance?"

First, let's again be perfectly clear. *No* form of investing is risk free. Even keeping your money under a mattress carries with it a certain amount of risk. But there is a reason banks lend money. It's a pretty sure bet they will be paid back. If they're not, they come after the borrower, sometimes in a big way. Foreclosure isn't fun. Now, think of yourself as the bank; that's what a debt partner is. You are lending on the asset—the property—and because you are lending at a low loan-to-value, you know that the property is (or will be) worth much more than what you have invested.

How much more? Typically, a debt partner should not lend more than 70 percent of the actual retail value—or in the case of a rehab, the after-repair value of a property.

As a debt partner, you also want to ask yourself, "Am I looking for quick profits or long term cash flow? Do I prefer to be one of many partners on a large apartment or commercial deal? or do I want to be the only lender on a single-family deal, or something between?" No matter what the property or exit strategy, as a debt partner your risk is low, and your rewards (return on investment) are also typically low compared to the equity partner (see chapter 8).

In the world of real estate investing, just as in any other type of investing, the higher the risk, the higher the reward. The difference with real estate is that the fall is not as fast. That is, because the real estate cycle is gradual (see chapter 4) it's easier to see the rises and falls coming. But, where investing in stocks can be much about speculation, the real estate investors who survived the last cycle know that speculation in real estate is a risk that many no longer need or desire to take. The investor can make solid, sustainable returns without speculation and very low risk, just by being prudent and diligent.

What You *Should* Expect as a Debt Partner

A debt partner is a lender. As a lender, you will be asked to provide some very specific and personal financial information:

- Proof of funds*
- Proof of funds liquidity*
- Commitment letter*
- Nonrefundable commitment deposit (not always requested)
- Depending on the type of investment, you may be required to complete an "accredited investor questionnaire."

What the REE will provide you once you are an approved investor:

- Property financials
- Property expectations
- Letter of intent to purchase (LOI) or purchase contract*
- General property information
- Exit strategy
- Due diligence or property condition report*
- Title and survey reports
- Deed of Trust* (at closing)
- Property insurance with you as additional insured (at closing)

The Private Money Loan

As a debt partner you will be providing a nonrecourse or trust deed loan. There are two types of loans, recourse and nonrecourse. *Recourse loans* are the types of loans most of us are familiar with. To qualify for this loan, every aspect of your finances, tax returns, financial history, property you own, etc. is considered. Why? So, that if you default, the lender has something to take from you and your credit can be destroyed. A *nonrecourse loan* is a loan based on the asset. What the asset earns is important—not what you earn. The asset's financial condition is important—not your financial condition.

*see Terms and Definitions

The typical private money investment is a nonrecourse loan, or a trust deed investment. Trust deed investing allows you to become the bank and lend your money secured by real estate. Most trust deed investments are short-term loans (with maturities between one and five years) made to real estate entrepreneurs on non-owner-occupied investment properties. This loan is based solely on the asset.

Debt Partner Basics

- Debt partners do not participate in profits or losses.
- Debt partnerships are most commonly offered on single-family or small multifamily buy-and-hold or flip properties.
- The loan is secured by real estate property as collateral to a non-owner real estate entrepreneur. Terms for these types of loans will vary by REE and will depend upon the experience level of the borrower, as well as the length of an investor's relationship with a particular REE. Therefore, there are really no hard-and-fast rules for the debt partner.
- Debt partners provide financing for up to 80 percent of the fair market value (FMV)—or in the case of after-repair value (ARV) of the property, 100 percent of the cost of the property—plus any repairs, including closing costs.
- Debt partners receive a promissory note, deed of trust, and insurance.
- Your entire investment is backed by the property.
- Terms are set by the REE and may be interest only, amortized, or simple interest—usually annualized.
- Single debt partner: invests up to 100 percent of required funding for a property or project
- Multiple debt partners: No more than ten debt partners invest up to 100 percent on a single property through fractional notes. A *fractional note* is simply a standard promissory note or deed of trust on a property where there are multiple lenders placed in first position. Regardless of the investment amount, the debt partners will have identical rights to lien position, foreclosure, and interest rate.

- Debt partners receive financial statements on a monthly, quarterly, or yearly basis, depending on the nature of the deal and exit strategy.

If you are interested in becoming a private lender—or, in other words, a professional debt partner—there are some great books on the subject of private lending. If you are considering a career as a private lender, consider reading these books and talking to a few private lenders. A good education in private lending is fundamental to offering your services to REEs and real estate investment companies.

Frequently Asked Questions

Q: What is a debt partner?

A: A debt partner is a private investor that lends money secured by real estate property as collateral to a non-owner real estate investor. Terms for these types of loans will vary, and may be based on the length of an investor's relationship with a particular debt partner. Therefore, there are really no hard-and-fast rules.

Unless you are in the private money lending business, the rules are made by the REE or real estate company.

Q: Why should someone become a debt partner?

A: Most real estate entrepreneurs are well aware that banks are very strict on lending and are not paying any yield for CDs or money market accounts. Unfortunately, as the limits on funding continues, the real estate investment market is heating up! Real estate prices were at their lowest prices in our lifetimes. Real estate entrepreneurs can buy and fix up properties that combine cash flow with low loan balances and plenty of equity in the properties. As a debt partner you can lend at rates significantly higher than what you are currently getting, and the REE obtains loans with very little hassle...a win-win for both!

Q: What is trust deed investing?

A: As a debt partner you are investing in a trust deed, which allows you to *become the bank* and lend your money secured by real estate. Most trust deed investments are short-term loans (maturities between one and five years) made to professional real estate investors on non-owner-occupied investment properties.

Banks are unwilling to make real estate loans unless they fit a very strict set of criteria. For this reason, the REE may have limited financing options available to them. Debt investing bridges the gap by either funding the down payment (providing a second position trust deed) or funding the entire property (first position trust deed).

Q: Is the private money loan being sought by an experienced and reputable real estate investment company?

A: Basically, is the real estate investment company you're working with a "fly-by-night" operation? or are they a reputable company run by highly regarded REEs with a track record of success? It shouldn't matter whether the REE is full-time or part-time. What is important is whether they treat it as a business or a hobby.

Q: Can I diversify my debt investing by lending on multiple properties at the same time?

A: A sound real estate investment company will only take on properties that make good financial sense for all parties. It may be a good idea if you have the opportunity to spread your funds out into multiple private loans to further diversify your private money loan portfolio by investing in properties with various exit strategies. Ask the real estate investment company you are working with if this is a possibility.

Q: What is the "LTV" of a private money loan?

A: "LTV" refers to *loan-to-value*. The higher the LTV, the higher the risk may be on a particular private money loan. Many REEs work on tight margins and buy properties at 80 percent and up. We recommend a maximum LTV of 80 percent on larger multifamily apartment properties that will be held for five years or more. We recommend a maximum LTV of 70 percent on smaller residential and commercial properties that are short-term (less than eighteen months) holds, usually "flips." This drastically increases the "wiggle room" of the overall transaction and ensures that the REE and his debt partner are protected as much as possible.

Q: Is my private money loan properly secured? What documents will I receive to show my position in the property?

A: This is a very important question to ask before you participate in a private money loan. Ask the real estate investment company what documents you will get before and after the transaction closes that show your protection and position in the property. Also, ask the company if the proper documents that place you as the "mortgagee" on the property will be filed with the county courthouse. Debt partners should expect to receive a full package of signed and recorded documents before and after the transaction takes place. These include, but may not be limited to, the filed trust deed/mortgage, disclosure statement, promissory note, and insurance binder. You also receive a complete loan package, including loan application, property report, property and title insurance, servicing agreement, and most importantly, a promissory note and recorded first or second mortgage in your name.

Q: Does the real estate investment company have proper insurance on the property naming me as a lienholder/additional insured on the property?

A: This is extremely important and often overlooked by first-time debt partners. A reputable real estate investment company will purchase proper insurance to cover the property and place you as the private money lender on the policy as the "additional insured/mortgagee/etc." to protect you and your investment. Debt partners should expect to be on the insurance policy to protect them and their investment in case of a catastrophic loss of the property. The real estate investment company should provide you with a copy of the insurance binder immediately after the close of the transaction.

Q: What kind of returns can debt partners expect?

A: Debt partners may start getting interest rates of 5 to 6 percent. As the relationship with the REE matures, higher returns are possible for trust deed investors, depending on their risk tolerance levels and when equity participation is available.

Q: Can I invest with my retirement funds?

A: Yes, there are corporations, trusts, pension plans, IRAs, and 401(k)s investing in trust deeds. A REE can help identify a self-directed custodian and guide you through the application/transfer process. These firms specialize in administering IRAs that are invested in alternative asset classes such as real estate, trust deeds, and commodities.

Q: How do I receive payments?

A: Payments may be received monthly, quarterly, or annually. This should be discussed and set up with the REE you are working with. In many cases, debt investor loans are served through a third-party servicing company and the REE never has access to your money. Money may be direct-deposited or wired to your bank account. As with any investment, you should receive statements or have online access to monitor your loan's performance.

Q: What is the margin of safety in a trust deed investment?

A: The margin of safety is the difference between the loan amount and the value of the underlying property. The golden rule of protecting your investment with trust deed investing is that if the REE has 20 percent or greater equity in the property, then the investment should not lose money even if the REE defaults on the loan. The debt partner can foreclose on the property and sell it to recoup the investment and potentially sell for a profit. A well-structured trust deed investment should always remain at or less than 70 to 80 percent loan-to-value.

If your are investing in the second position deed of trust, as a rule of thumb, don't invest more than 30 percent loan-to-value.

Q: Trust deed investing seems too good to be true. What is the catch?

A: The risk-adjusted returns of trust deed investments are very attractive. First of all, these investments have limited liquidity and therefore cannot be converted into cash quickly. Secondly, there is risk involved, the most obvious of which being that if the borrower defaults and the debt partner forecloses, the property may need to be spruced up to recoup investment. Properly valuing the property up front and structuring the deal with a high enough margin of safety limits this risk. That being said, as a debt partner, investing in trust deeds can be done in a very safe and secure manner. The debt partner needs to be armed with the proper knowledge through good due diligence.

Q: During the financial crisis, there were billions of dollars in losses. How are new investments in private loans any safer?

A: During the financial crisis, real estate values dropped 40 percent or more. Lenders' losses were exacerbated by a number of factors including the following:

1. Many residential loans were made at 85 percent or even 100 percent of market value, so that the margin of safety for the lenders was nonexistent.

2. Many loans were made to borrowers with poor credit or no income verification.

3. Commercial real estate loans funded for development of high-rise buildings and subdivisions only made sense under very optimistic assumptions.

Today's real estate loan investments are not immune from losses. However, the risk is lower because another 40 percent drop in values from today's much lower values is unlikely. Secondly, experienced REEs limit their loan amount to 70-80 percent of current market value.

Q: Why don't major Wall Street firms offer trust deed investments?

A: In short, Wall Street firms cannot make enough money from trust deed investments to make it worth their while. The size of each investment and the work involved in creating each investment property combine to make this business "nonscalable" from their perspective. It is the absence of huge amounts of capital in this market that explains the strong risk-adjusted returns available to those willing and able to participate in the market.

Q: What is the minimum investment for trust deed investments?

A: The minimum investment amount is typically $25,000, but some REEs may require $100,000 or more. However, fractional investments aren't always available on each trust deed; single investors are awarded priority over fractional investors. As a practical matter, we believe it is better to invest a larger amount spread across several transactions to diversify your investment in trust deeds.

Q: Who are the borrowers and how can they afford to pay double-digit interest rates?

A: The borrowers are savvy real estate investors who are planning to make a very large return when they buy a foreclosure and sell for a profit, or who simply need a fast loan with the minimal paperwork that banks require. These borrowers can afford to pay higher rates, even though the loan is well-secured, because the borrowers are typically aiming to make an annualized return of 15 percent or more on their investments. Paying the debt partner a lower return (relative to their projected returns) allows them to enhance the yields they earn on their cash investment.

Q: So how can a debt partner profit?

A: Debt partnering is fast becoming the best solution for many investors to earn yield in today's market. Passive investors can earn a great return on investments that beat the money managers and inflation while creating cash flow. Private investor lending overlooks credit and income issues and gives knowledgeable REEs the ability to take advantage of low real estate prices.

Chapter 8:

The Equity Partnership

We have spent a chapter covering the benefits of being a debt partner. Now let's cover equity investing and why, even though the risk may be greater, the reward can also be significantly improved.

The equity partner is a true partner in the property investment. He or she is a partner in an entity (typically a Limited Liability Company) that owns the property, and is entitled to a proportion of the distributable profits of the partnership as well as the tax benefits.

He or she may be the only partner, or may be one of many partners who share in the profits and losses of an investment as part of the LLC fraction or a syndication (see "A Quick Word about Syndications," at the end of the chapter). Equity investing has significant benefits for the seasoned private money partner that can make it far more appealing than the debt partnership. Whether in a syndication or a simple LLC partnership, each equity partner becomes a passive participant in the ownership.

Prospective private money partners should be prequalified and prescreened before receiving opportunities via the LLC fraction or private placement memorandum. Investments are not for everyone and are typically not offered to the general public. Once a private investor is invited in to the private equity group investment, the investor has the opportunity to participate with an organized group of likeminded accredited and sophisticated investor partners in the ownership of a revenue-generating property.

As with the debt partner, the equity partner may participate in short-term investments with increased profits at a higher risk, or long-term investments with steady wealth-generating cash flow at a lower risk. Whether used for wealth-generating or wealth-preservation, the equity partnership is a means to create both.

Let's talk about the short-term investments first. Short-term investments are more exciting, but can come with more risk.

A Sample Flip Scenario

We recently completed a residential Flip in a desirable part of town. We found a property that appeared to meet all of our criteria. We found a single equity investor to invest 70 percent of the after-repair value. We did all of the work. The investor's money did her work for her, and the net profit would be split fifty-fifty. At the time we bought the property, values in the neighborhood told us we could sell the house for $200,000 (about 10 percent below the average sale). A sale at that price would mean a profit of just over $46,000.

Due to some delays in the rehab work we didn't sell the property until six months later. This increased the holding costs and the market value dropped by 5 percent.

We sold the property for $189,900 and the net profit was $37,000. Because we had a fifty-fifty split, our investor made $18,500 or 13 percent on her investment in just six months, or an annualized return of 26 percent! If property values had increased rather than decreased 5 percent, her profit as an equity partner would have increased to $28,000 or 19.5 percent, annualized at almost 40 percent! Had our investor opted for the safer debt investment, she would have received about 8 percent on her investment no matter what the profit. Less risk...less reward!

A word of caution: profits from flips are considered active income by the IRS and are taxed at the highest rate.

This case study is not to suggest that you can make these profits. It's just to show you what a short-term equity investment could look like.

Now let's look at where the real wealth can be found: long-term equity investing in multifamily and commercial real estate.

Long-Term Equity Investing

1. Predictable Revenue

A property's revenue is derived from rents paid for the use of leased properties. A strong property management team will focus on attracting only the most suitable occupants to the properties and bind them to carefully structured lease agreements, contracted for long periods of time with staggered renewal dates. These practices in turn generate consistent cash flow for investor partners.

2. Capital Appreciation

By making improvements, the property values are increased through the value-add process. By increasing rents or occupancy rates, higher levels of stable monthly distributions are generated. When properties are refinanced or sold, the proceeds can be used to acquire additional properties to further increase value and wealth preservation.

3. Steady Cash Flow

One of the greatest advantages of real estate investments is that they generate steady, strong, partly tax-sheltered cash flow and provide distributions. With the other advantages real estate has to offer, few other forms of investments can be bought with the same kind of steady cash-flow return combined with the appreciation of the investment over time.

4. Tax Efficiency

Distributions to investor partners are treated more favorably than other investments from a tax perspective because a significant portion of distributions is not considered income. This is due to the flow-through of expenses and depreciation. Furthermore, the capital appreciation is deferred from taxation until the assets are sold.

5. Total Return

A property's combination of revenue (from rents), capital gains (resulting from increased property values), principal pay-down (from renters paying down loans), and tax savings (thanks to the investment's special flow-through structure) may provide consistent, stable returns.

6. Hedge Against Inflation

Notwithstanding cyclical variations due to supply-and-demand imbalances, in the long run, rents, values, and the replacement cost of real estate improvements rise in line with inflation. Multifamily assets also tend to have shorter-term leases which can adjust to current market conditions much faster than other investments such as office or retail assets. This makes real estate investing as an equity partner a particularly effective hedge against inflation, and should be a key component in any well-diversified investment portfolio.

The Best Part about Being an Equity Investor

Most REEs offer equity investment opportunities on real estate assets to be held for three to five years or longer. Typically, once an asset has been held for a minimum of three years, it will be refinanced, the investor's principal will be paid back, and a preferred interest may continue to be paid for a predetermined period or until the property is sold.

What does that mean for you?

You get your principal investment back—and can reinvest it in another property—and continue to make money on the first property. Can your stocks and mutual funds do that?

Equity Investor Expectations

Equity investors come in many sizes. You may be a single limited partner, part of a larger limited partnership syndication, or part of a TIC (Tenants In Common) ownership.

In any case, once it has been established that you qualify for the investment, you will be required to fill out a subscription agreement. This is an application by an investor to join a limited partnership. In most cases, the investor will have to fill out a form created by the REE evaluating the investor's further suitability for the investment in the partnership. Not all subscription agreements are created equal. They are designed to protect the REE and are customized to follow the rules and regulations of the state in which the property is located. Once the subscription agreement has been completed, it is reviewed by the real estate company or REE to determine whether the investor is accredited, sophisticated, or not prepared to invest. An accredited investor may be invited to invest more money than the sophisticated investor.

When a property deal goes under contract, each qualified investor receives an executive summary of the property and meets with the REE to discuss the opportunity. The REE will then provide the private investor with the private placement memorandum and the private investor will pledge the investment amount. The REE may or may not require a refundable or nonrefundable deposit as a guarantee at this time. It's important to keep in mind that no cash changes hands. Funds are either wired or direct transferred, or a check is deposited in to an escrow account held by the title company, closing attorney, or the REE's real estate attorney.

A Quick Word about Syndication

In their simplest form, a real estate syndication is simply the pooling of money from numerous investors and organizing these funds as a whole into real estate projects. The moneys contributed can be used as an equity investment to a real estate project in addition to a commercial loan secured by a mortgage or trust deed to fund the bulk of the cost and development of the project. Investing in a real estate syndicate is essentially investing in a commercial real estate venture. Common examples would be the purchase of land to develop a residential apartment complex or an industrial park for small-scale manufacturing of items.

Investing in a real estate syndication requires significant due diligence in looking into the pros and cons of the potential investment. There are never any guarantees that the venture will be profitable. As such, it is highly recommended that individuals considering investing in a real estate syndication do a thorough background search of the REE, real estate company, and its partners involved in getting the project off the ground, and consult with their financial advisors as to the merits of the investment and inherent risks. The benefits of investing in a real estate syndication is that a person can end up owning a small percentage in the real property being offered without having to be involved in the day-to-day management of the project.

How Real Estate Syndication Makes Money

The person who desires to create a real estate syndication must comply with the laws of the state where the real estate syndication is to be created and operated. The syndicator of such a venture usually receives compensation for locating the property to be purchased, doing the due diligence for its acquisition and intended development, and getting the purchase to close. Private investors in the transaction typically pay the syndicator's fee based upon a percentage of the costs of the transaction when the targeted property is acquired.

Another way a syndicator makes money in a real estate syndication is as a management fee, typically based upon a percentage of gross revenue on a yearly basis. For example, if there has been an apartment complex constructed and owned by the syndication, the gross profits for property and/or asset management of the apartment complex would be paid to the syndicator for collecting rental money, maintaining the complex, paying insurance, taxes, and making repairs.

The final way for a syndicator to make money through a real estate syndicate is by investing in the project itself, which is typically the case. The REE syndicator typically receives dividends along with the private investors, paid quarterly on his or her investment, besides maintaining an ownership interest in the syndicated project.

Let's say that you are part of a group of private investors in a syndication formed by a real estate company. The REE acquires a building for $1,000,000—all cash, no mortgage. The private investors put up the entire amount, which includes the real estate acquisition or syndication fee. After all of the expenses have been paid, including an asset management fee, the property generates $120,000 in profit its first year. As private investors you could be entitled to a preferred interest payment first. Let's assume that it is a preferred interest rate of 6 percent. That means that the pool of private investors would get $60,000 in interest first out of that $120,000 profit (6 percent of $1,000,000). The remaining $60,000 would be split between the REE and the private investor pool at whatever percentage you previously agreed upon. That could be a 50–50 split, or it could be a 75–25 split, with your investors getting the larger portion.

So, with a 6 percent preferred rate of return and a 50–50 split, the private investors would have made $60,000 in interest and another

$30,000 from its equity participation in the cash flow from the property. This would equate to a 9 percent cash-on-cash return. Plus, as an equity partner you would still have an equity percentage in the appreciation of the property, so there is still an opportunity for you to make more money on the back end once the property is refinanced or sold.

As the syndicator, the REE was able to participate in a deal with little money out of his or her own pocket. The REE will have been paid through an acquisition or syndication fee, asset management fee, and an additional $30,000 in cash flow. In addition, he or she will still have a 50 percent stake in any future equity appreciation in the property.

Concerns Over a Real Estate Syndication

Many states in this country through their departments of corporations oversee real estate syndications in order to protect the public as well as potential investors, requiring yearly reporting by the syndicator on each real estate syndication. In the past there have been many fraudulent syndication projects where investors have lost significant sums of money by investing in purportedly reputable syndication projects. Investing in a real estate syndication should be done only after a thorough investigation of the people heading the syndication and the project.

Frequently Asked Questions

Q: What is nonrecourse lending and how does that affect me as an investor?

A: Nonrecourse means that the borrower and private investors are not personally liable for the asset. In other words, the lender cannot pursue the borrowers' and private investors' other assets, affect their credit, or place any personal liability on the borrowers and private investors involved in the property or project.

Q: What is my liability on a loan?

A: In some cases, the REE may require an additional sponsor to obtain a larger commercial loan. The sponsor is typically an investor who provides additional "confidence" for the bank by providing his or her personal financial statement and any additional required documents to demonstrate "credit worthiness," and subsequently provides greater security on the loan. As a sponsor, you may take on greater risk, and consequently this will increase your reward in the form of a bigger ROI. Remember this: all equity partners are not created equal. Profit is based on risk.

Q: In many cases, the REE and equity partners make the down payment of 25–30 percent with the remaining funds from a financial institution. What happens when the loan is a recourse loan versus a nonrecourse loan?

A: If you are asked to participate as an equity partner on a smaller property, it may be likely that any lending by a bank or mortgage company is based on the credit worthiness of all partners involved in the transaction. This places greater risk on all because everyone becomes financially responsible. This greater risk demands greater reward, but also demands greater trust in your relationship with the real estate entrepreneur. It is critical that you discuss the pros and cons with the REE you are working with.

Q: What are the equity investor funds used for?

A: Money obtained through equity investments are typically used for anything the bank (institutional) lender does not cover. This may include (but not be limited to)

- Earnest money deposit after the purchase agreement (contract) has been signed
- Down payment
- Closing costs
- Loan fees
- Operating capital
- Holding and carrying costs (when used for flipping)
- Full property price (if a lender isn't being used)

Q: I've heard that large apartment properties not only have property management but also have asset management. What is that? Who pays for that?

A: Property management handles the day-to-day affairs of the property. Asset management is a single point of accountability for all aspects of commercial real estate. When it comes to overseeing property managers, operating procedures, and capital improvements planning, asset management handles the nuts and bolts of all financial facets. It provides for open-book reporting—from annual business plans and hold/sell analyses to monthly operating reports—to keep you informed of your position. The cost of asset management is typically shared among the investors.

Q: Do I have a choice of when I get my money back?

A: Returns on your principal will vary with the terms and length of the initial investment. The REE may, under some circumstances, return your principal early; however, that is on a case-by-case basis and may be subject to a penalty. Make sure that the money you invest isn't "household" money. In many cases you must be either an accredited or sophisticated investor and prove that the money you invest is not needed for living expenses.

The real estate investments with a REE are private transactions in physical properties around the world. The investments are not traded on public stock exchanges and cannot be easily sold or traded.

Different properties have different expected "hold periods." A hold period is the anticipated time investors will be involved with the investment until it is resold or the loan is paid off, and range from less than six months to greater than five years. It is important to read the investor documents for a deeper understanding of the hold period for each investment.

In some cases, when you are a fractional investor in an LLC you may sell your fraction to another member of the LLC or outside investor. You can expect to sell your "share" at a loss, or for less than your initial investment. Discuss this with the REE before you invest.

As an investor, you will receive a return on your investment when the company distributes money. Money is typically distributed on two occasions: 1) when investors receive their share of the profits (as equity investors) or their agreed-upon interest (as loan investors) or 2) the property is sold.

This can be a touchy subject for many REEs. In most cases, it can be difficult if not impractical to return principal before the end of the agreed term. Most REE will make every effort to work with you. Part of the Subscription Agreement and the Private Placement Memorandum is to clarify all of the terms and provide both of you with a legally binding agreement.

Q: How do you pay the dividends on my investment?

A: Returns are paid based on the nature of the investment. You may invest in short-term and long-term investment properties. Typically, long-term investments are paid quarterly, and short-term may be paid at the end of the term, or every X months.

It's important to understand that the REE is usually the managing partner on the investment and is in control of when dividends are distributed. As the limited partner, you are subject to the terms of the agreement. You may receive quarterly financial statements or summary reports, and should always receive year-end statements and any notifications of changes. This is a very important discussion that the REE will have with you.

Q: What is a "preferred interest" payment?

A: Preferred interest is the amount paid on the investment before dividing up the cash flow.

As an example—say the private investors provide $1 million down payment on a $3 million property. They get 50 percent of the cash flow and profits and a 5 percent preferred interest. This means the investors get 5 percent of $1 million, or $50,000. The property cash-flows $120,000 a year. Subtract $50,000 and the private investors and REE get 50 percent each of the remaining $70,000, or $35,000. The investors get a total of $85,000 a year, or a cash-on-cash return of 8.5 percent per year. If there is no preferred interest, the entire $120,000 in cash flow would be split. In this case, the investors would get $60,000, or 6 percent cash-on-cash return. The preferred interest makes the deal more appealing to the private investor.

The REE will often structure deals to make them as appealing as possible to the equity partners.

Remember, in addition to the cash-on-cash return, you receive depreciation on your taxes, as well as additional profits as the property appreciates, rents increase, and at sale.

Q: Will I get to deduct depreciation?

A: As an equity partner you are a limited partner in the property or project. As such, you are entitled to deductions including depreciation. This is why the year-end statement is so important. Your accountant can provide you the details.

Q: Will I actually own the property?

A: Because you are a limited partner, you have limited ownership. You will receive limited profits from the property and your liability toward its debts is legally limited to the extent of your investment. As an equity partner, you will typically own shares or membership interest in a limited partnership solely set up for each individual project or property.

Q: When can I expect to get my investment back?

A: Depending on the property type that you invest in, the dividends or profits you receive may be paid out monthly, quarterly, or in one lump sum when the project is complete. Typically, in the case of existing cash-flowing assets, investors will begin to receive checks in the form of dividends three to six months after their original investment.

Q: Will I participate in any decisions?

A: The REE is the general partner and subsequently has full

management control. Equity partners, as the limited partners, may take part in decisions only to the extent that the general partner offers this ability. Talk to the REE you are working with.

Q: What happens if a deal is oversubscribed?

A: Each deal is first-come, first-served. The REE may collect only the amount of funding needed for the deal in the subscription agreement. Therefore, it's very important that if you like a deal, you let the REE know *right away*, or you may have to wait for the next one.

Q: What is real estate syndication?

A: Real estate syndication is "crowdfunding for real estate" before crowdfunding for real estate ever existed. In their simplest forms, both syndication and crowdfunding involve pooling capital with other individuals for a common purpose or a common goal. In real estate, that common purpose is the purchase of a real property, a physical building you can see and touch.

The difference between real estate syndication and crowdfunding is introducing the Internet as a distribution vehicle and the use of technology to allow a wider range of investors to contribute capital to a real estate transaction. While syndications have historically been completed offline, crowdfunding is facilitated largely through online means, allowing investors to invest in real estate from the comfort of their living room and the convenience of their smartphone or iPad.

Q: Why do people engage in real estate syndication?

A: Access to deal flow is the biggest reason investors participate in real estate syndication or crowdfunding for real estate. Not every investor has the time to search and underwrite hundreds of properties to find a gem to acquire. Since there are thousands of real estate companies all over the United States that do this for a living, getting involved through real estate syndication enables investors to access this deal flow and gives them the ability to invest in real estate without the hassles of property management.

Q: Who is involved with real estate syndication?

A: The first ingredient for a real estate syndication is a "syndicator" or "sponsor." This individual or company is in charge of finding, acquiring, and managing the real estate. They have a history of real estate experience and the ability to underwrite and complete due diligence on the real estate.

Q: How can I be part of a syndication?

A: First you need to find a REE who offers syndication for property investing. Most REEs that invest in larger multifamily and commercial properties are able to set up syndications to offer the opportunities to more private investors. Because syndications can be complicated to set up, the REE would do this through an SEC attorney on his or her team. There are SEC rules and regulations in regard to who and how many investors can be a part of a real estate syndicate.

The size of a syndication is limited, so, if you are interested in an opportunity that the REE presents, it is important that you are able to make a speedy decision.

Q: What if I no longer want to be in the syndication?

A: Being part of a syndication allows you the opportunity to be "bought out." Many private investors have the opportunity to sell their interest in a real estate syndication down the road to a willing buyer or even to the syndicator. There may be an additional fee or you may have to sell your interest at a discount. Discuss this with the REE syndicator.

Q: Lets say the worst-case scenario happens and the property is foreclosed…what happens to my investment?

A: There is always a risk that you may lose your investment. Because savvy real estate entrepreneurs care more about the investors' money than their own, they will do whatever is possible to make sure the investment isn't lost. The lender doesn't want to sell the property for less than the loan. It doesn't want to manage and maintain it until another buyer can be found. As a result, REEs may have some options. They can try to work out a modification of the loan that allows them to catch up with the payments. This is common with commercial properties. REEs will attempt a modification as soon as possible, before the foreclosure process has gone too far. They may also speak with a lawyer about filing for bankruptcy. But first and foremost, they will make sure that all investors are informed and aware of what is happening.

This brings us to our next and extremely important topic of transparency.

Chapter 9:

Transparency

Transparency is an essential part in the real estate entrepreneur–private money partner relationship.

Let's first define the general term.

Relationship—
The way in which two or more concepts, objects, or people are connected, or the state of being connected.

Now here is the term as defined—adding "business."

Business relationship—
A formal contractual relationship established to provide for regular banking or brokerage or business services.

Now let's define relationship transparency this way:

Relationship transparency is an individual's subjective perception of being informed about the relevant actions and properties of the other party in the interaction.

So, relationship transparency contributes to the overall success of a business relationship. It delivers value, increases satisfaction, and ultimately leads to favorable outcomes.

Transparency is more than just knowing "what's going on." It's about knowing the why and how behind it. This starts long before you start receiving your quarterly financial statements or property summary reports. It starts with the initial offering. It starts with knowing that the REE is in full control of every aspect of the deal, from initial structuring to continuing asset management. The REE must be able to convey that control through providing information as it's needed, organizing and managing the project, and assisting the investor in making the right decisions based on his or her investment needs and desires.

Four Key Factors

Starting with the initial opportunity, the REE must cover four key factors when presenting an opportunity (deal) to a private investor before the investor can consider becoming a private money partner.

1. Project or Property

What is the project or property the investor is providing capital for? Not only do you need to know where it is or how much it costs, but also find out why the REE thinks it's a good investment.

Expect more than pictures and a few graphs. The REE should be able to provide a full-spectrum spreadsheet with the property financials.

2. Partners

Who are the key partners behind the project? What you are looking for here is not just names of everyone the REE has ever worked with, but specifically who is on the team for the property he or she is presenting to you.

Who is putting the deal together? Usually, the REE you are working with is structuring the deal. You'll want a little background on his or her education, training, and of course experience. Remember, the REE will often refer to the experience of his or her team. That's OK, but REEs should have their own experience, too!

What is the track record of the partners? What experience do they have? You should know everyone who is actively involved with the project and how all of the partners are qualified to make the project a success.

3. Financing

What is the total cost of the project? That question is simple enough...right? Not really. There are often costs associated with the deal that may not be so obvious. You should expect to see soft costs, which may include an acquisition fee, syndication fee, professional fees, due diligence costs (inspections, reports), and construction costs if any rehab or capital expenditures are made.

How much debt and how much equity is there? What you are looking for here is how much is expected to be financed and how much the REE will need to raise from private investors.

What is the investors' return and reward for their risk? You should look for what your effective passive income is at the end of each year. Sometimes this may be cumulative over a period of three to five years or more. You'll want to know how you will be paid and when. The REE should discuss things like cash-on-cash return, cash flow (before and after tax), internal rate of return, and other metrics to help you understand what your return on investment will be.

What are the tax consequences? This is something you will want to discuss with your accountant. The REE should provide you with the information you will need to bring your accountant.

Who is the accounting firm? You may want to sit down with the real estate entrepreneurs' accountant to review the deal.

What is the property exit? Is this a buy-and-hold? If so, for how long? Will the REE refinance in three, five, or seven years and pay back the principal at that time? or will you have to wait for a sale? Is this a flip (single family) or reposition (commercial/multi-family). This information will aid you and the REE in determining how much you should invest.

How the project will make money? A property or project can make money in more than one way. But just as important is how it could lose money. You should have a clear understanding of the average expected assumptions. In other words, what are the expected risks?

The REE should be able to answer these two key questions:

- How soon will private investors get their initial investment back?
- What is the expected ROI for private investors?

The bottom line: the financing structure and terms should be attractive to the private investor.

4. Management

Who is running the day-to-day operations? In most cases of multifamily and commercial property deals, an outsourced property management company does the management. You'll want to know something about them.

- What is their experience, and the experience of the team?
- What is their background?
- What makes them vital to the success of this project?

For smaller portfolios, asset management is typically handled by the REE and his or her real estate accountant. As the size of the property portfolio increases, the savvy REE will either form an asset management company or hire a reliable third-party asset management company to report the financials. In either case, the REE has a responsibility to the private money partners to maintain control.

Now, let's look at the basic steps of a real estate deal for a large multifamily or commercial property.

The Groundwork

Before the transaction even begins, the REE has spent days, weeks, or even months researching a market to determine efficacy of the deal in that location. The REE will consider, based on the exit strategy, various metrics to determine what strategy will make the biggest ROI. Research may include—but is not limited to—local economics, job outlook, demographics, availability of housing, types of housing available, fair market rents, income levels, topography, highways and interstates, paths of progress, infrastructure, and more. Remember the real estate market cycle?

Analyzing the general real estate market will also include the following: how long it takes similar properties to sell, how much they sell for compared to the asking price, and how much the property could sell for in one, three, or five years or more.

Can you see how this is more than just picking a nice-looking building?

The Cash Flow or Flip Analysis

The most critical step of the groundwork is the initial analysis. The REE will look at the income versus expenses. Does the property provide the cash flow necessary to provide a solid, consistent rate of return for the investor? If the property is a reposition, how long will it take to make the improvements and reposition? What are the costs to do the improvements? Other things the REE must consider include how the property compares to other local properties. What are the fair market rents? What are the sales comparisons?

Next, if the location fits the REE's parameters, he or she will build a team that will consist of (at the very least) a real estate broker, attorney, and appraiser. Other members are added as they become necessary. If the property is going to cash flow, the next team member would be the property management company. If the property is going to be rehabbed and repositioned for refinance or sold, the next team member would be a general contractor.

The property is further analyzed using information from the seller. This usually includes a marketing package with twelve months of rental and expense information. This is just to get the basic evaluation of the property to determine at what price it becomes a good deal. Additionally, lenders are sourced to determine what kind of financing is available for the property.

A letter of intent is submitted. This nonbinding document simply lets the seller know that the REE is interested in buying the property. It provides a basic outline of desired terms. The LOI can go through several rounds of counters over days or weeks before there is a preliminary agreement.

A property plan, also called a property business plan or marketing plan, is prepared for the private investors once the terms of the LOI are agreed upon. This initial offering is to share the opportunity with the investors that qualify.

The property "goes under contract." The REE and the attorney complete the purchase and sales agreement contract and submit it to the seller. The seller will have a limited period of time to review and agree. It's not entirely unusual at this point for further negotiations to take place for several weeks. Upon "ratification" (both seller and buyer have agreed and signed), the contract, also called the purchase and sales agreement, is executed and the earnest money deposit (EMD) is placed in escrow with the buyer's or seller's attorney. Now "let the games begin!"

The REE goes back to the previously sourced candidates for private investing to share the terms of the deal and provide all of the details to the private investors participating in the transaction. Any new investors must fill out and sign an investor questionnaire before they can participate, to determine what type of investors they are and what properties or strategy best meets their needs. The real estate entrepreneur structures the deal, begins work with his or her SEC, real estate, and business attorneys, and begins the due diligence process on the property. The attorneys prepare the private placement memorandum or LLC documents and commitment letters for private investors who will become private money partners. In addition, there will be operating agreements and subscriber agreements.

The Due Diligence

Due diligence is broken down into three basic parts.

- Financial due diligence
- Physical due diligence
- Legal due diligence

These are completed by the REE and his or her team of attorneys, accountants, and property management. All three are vital and imperative. If one component of any one of these three elements cannot be determined, is incomplete, has errors, or any other issues— it's back to the negotiating table at the end of the due diligence.

It's during this due diligence period that loan packages are submitted to lenders that have been previously contacted, and final commitments are received from private money partners.

The REE will continue to be in contact with the private investors to update them on the timeline and progress of the deal. There may be several phone meetings with each individual investor to answer questions or address issues that may have come up.

Once a written commitment has been received from the lending institution and the private partners to finance the deal, and the final price and terms are negotiated one final time, due diligence is signed off.

Closing is set up, all funding from private investors has been placed in escrow, closing documents are reviewed by the attorney, and preparations are made for the physical, financial, and legal transfer of the property.

It's important to understand that the time span between private investor funding and finalizing the deal may be several weeks. During this period the interest on the investment may be minimal. All of this should be detailed in the private money partner agreement.

If the deal "dies" for any reason, the investor funds are typically returned with interest as agreed in the private money partner agreement. Be sure you understand this agreement completely. Although most real estate entrepreneurs will avoid contracts full of legalese, you may still want to have your attorney review it. If you have any concerns, you should discuss them with the REE.

A final word: the deal may be terminated at any time during this process for any reason. Until the deal is closed, anything can happen.

Don't expect the REE to advise you of the details to each and every step in the process, but do expect an update with every major event.

Post Closing

Once the property has closed, the private money partner will typically receive quarterly financial updates and a year-end statement. This will continue as long as you are part of the investment. The REE may include other ways to maintain transparency. These may include communications through periodic calls, investor group meetings, newsletters, and emails. But the most important report is the financial statement.

The word "transparent" can be used to describe high-quality financial statements. The term has quickly become a part of business vocabulary. Dictionaries offer many definitions for the word, but those synonyms relevant to financial reporting are: "easily understood," "very clear," "frank," and "candid."

When financial statements are not transparent, private money partners can never be sure about a property's real fundamentals and true risk. Private money partners should seek disclosure and simplicity. Each and every property or project you invest in will have its own financial statement and updates. These statements will include simple basics— income versus expenses, including capital expenses and any losses. The more REEs say about where they are making money and how they are spending their resources, the more confident investors can be about their fundamentals.

When the private investor is investing in any type of property or project, transparency makes analysis easier and therefore lowers the risk. That way you are less likely to face unpleasant surprises.

The "Guarantee"

A word about guarantees: there are none.

While the word "guarantee" sounds warm and fuzzy, it is illegal for anyone to guarantee the returns on any debt or equity investment. Private money lending and partnering with reputable real estate investment companies is a preferred choice of investment for many of the nation's wealthy because of its higher returns and predictable consistency; however, if a REE "guarantees" your return you should run the other way. This law is the same one that prevents financial planners from "guaranteeing" stocks, mutual funds, or any investment product. While they may be relatively safe investments when chosen correctly, real estate investments cannot be and are not guaranteed.

While private money investments cannot be "guaranteed," they are among the most consistent and predictable ways to earn higher returns, and they are backed by low loan-to-value real estate, which provides an extra layer of "security" that traditional stocks do not provide. In other words, considering the potential returns on investment, real estate is among the safest investments on the planet.

Frequently Asked Questions

Q: Will I be notified of how my investment is doing?

A: You should always expect full transparency. The REE you work with should be able to outline a plan of how and when you will be updated on your investment.

Q: How can I know that the REE is being transparent about the property I've invested in?

A: Communication is the most important aspect of transparency. This communication may come in different forms, but typically you should get (at the very least) a year-end statement for your tax return. We suggest that if you are not receiving at least quarterly communications from the REE, that you should contact him or her! If you believe your REE is hiding something, you may consider calling the property management company or on-site property manager. Do a little "secret shopping" and ask them about the property as if you were a prospective renter.

In most cases the REE has the best of intentions, but when things go wrong you may stop hearing from him or her. This should be your first indication that there may be a problem. If you have been receiving monthly communications and then three months go by without a word, there may be some news that the REE doesn't want you to hear. In our opinion, there is no excuse for not communicating good or bad news. Lack of trust can only hurt the REE–private money partner relationship.

Q: I get a check once a quarter, but I never get any financial statements. What can I do?

A: Have a heart-to-heart with the REE. This is a relationship business and you should have a relationship with the REE that fosters trust and transparency. Let him or her know you want a financial statement with each check. The REE may suggest a property summary, which is a general accounting of the property, but not as detailed. This should be sufficient, but you should require a year-end financial statement for tax purposes.

Q: The financial statements I get from the companies I have stock in are so complicated I need my accountant to interpret them. Would a property financial statement be easier to read?

A: That depends on the real estate company. Financial statements are typically prepared by an accountant and by nature could be complex. In most cases, in an effort to simplify, property financial statements for a single property are easy to read and understand. If you are having difficulty, contact the REE and discuss it with him or her.

Q: What should a property financial statement include?

A: The financial statement should include income and expenses as well as a summary of "events." Events could include capital improvements, insurance loss, and a general history over the past month, quarter, and year.

Q: I don't get a financial statement; I get a property summary. Is there a difference?

A: The financial statement is a full accounting of the property, and usually will include a property summary. The property summary alone may not include a detailed breakdown of income and expenses. As stated previously, you should receive, at the very least, a year-end financial statement to provide to your bookkeeper or accountant for tax preparation.

Q: Are there any fees for private money partners?

A: This will vary with the REE and the investment type. In some cases there may be certain asset management fees that are shared among the private money partners (equity and debt partners). These fees may run anywhere from 1 to 3 percent of your investment per year for administrative and legal expenses, as well as ongoing reporting and communications such as tracking the project, getting timely updates, and ensuring that your money is returned in a timely and appropriate manner.

Chapter 10:

Case Studies

Josh and Marie B.—fifteen years to retirement, large 401(k) and IRAs—not accredited but sophisticated

Josh and Marie are both in information technology. He is an IT project manager, she a security specialist. Their kids are grown and off to college. They have several years before retirement and have watched their portfolio shrink during the recession. They love their jobs and have been quite successful. At one time they had considered investing in real estate and own a home that they, by default, rent out. After getting a bit of real estate training they realized this business wasn't for them, but they like the idea of investing without the "headache" of actually having to deal with the work.

Josh met a REE through a business networking event he was invited to by a friend. After meeting with the REE, he and Marie realized that investing with her was a great option that they hadn't previously considered. The REE, Cheryl, explained her strategy and business plan. She already had several properties and was considering a small apartment property in a nearby city. She explained the pros and cons to the property, and told Josh and Marie the merits of equity investing and debt investing. After determining their ability to invest by having them fill out an "investor questionnaire," she offered an opportunity to them. Cheryl offered a debt partnership at 7 percent annualized for five years. The investment was $75000. They would not be owners but lenders on a second mortgage with a bank in first position. After meeting with an attorney who explained the entire process, Josh and Marie wrote a check that was deposited in an escrow account at closing. Josh and Marie would receive a quarterly check for the next five years and make over $25,000 on their investment.

Ed L.—Oil money, accredited investor

As an accredited investor, Ed had a great deal of experience in investing in the oil business and stocks, but had never tried private investing in real estate. After consulting with his advisor and friend who also happened to invest in real estate, he decided to give it a shot. His advisor knew of a local real estate entrepreneur who worked in large multifamily and commercial retail properties in various markets around the country. After an introduction and several meetings, Ed decided it was time to "take the plunge."

Jim and his partner, Sarah, had two properties that they felt fit Ed's profile, and presented him with an executive summary for each. These included a cost analysis, five-year pro forma, and details about the property and investment strategy. After some lengthy discussions about Ed's risk tolerance, one of the properties was chosen as the best fit. This property would be purchased using a private placement memorandum, as required by the SEC, and each investor would have to invest a minimum of $100,000. All documentation was prepared by Jim and Sarah's SEC attorney and real estate attorney. The total equity investment would be 30 percent of the property purchase price, and the equity investors would receive a 4 percent preferred rate plus a percentage of the cash flow, depreciation, appreciation, and profits at sale.

Ed receives a quarterly dividend payment with a statement, and receives a year-end tax statement. In addition, he can opt in to a monthly investor call to update all investors on the "state of the property."

Jim and Sarah know the value in having a solid, experienced team. Because they under promise and over perform, their private money partners continue to reinvest with them. As a private investor, Ed knows the value in working with an experienced team and plans to continue his partnership with Jim and Sarah.

Esther S.—retired school teacher, always interested in real estate investing but afraid to go on her own. (She also lost a lot of her IRA in "the crash," but has a good pension.)

Although Esther thought she might try real estate investing, she just didn't like the idea of dealing with tenants, and flipping just seemed like too much work. As a teacher, she understood the importance of an education, and so she did what she could to learn as much as she could about real estate investing. After attending a few local investment clubs she made a few connections with some local real estate entrepreneurs. They discussed with her the various exit strategies they used, and after several meetings she decided to work with Rachel and her husband Rick. Although they didn't have a great deal of experience, they were very knowledgeable and she appreciated the time they had taken for a solid education in real estate investing. Having an experienced team behind them didn't hurt, either!

Rachel and Rick had been investing in single-family rentals for a couple of years and had recently just completed their first two flips. Both flips had been with private money lenders, and this sounded like what Esther wanted to do. They offered her a 6 percent annualized rate (twice what she had been getting) for a 65 percent loan-to-value on a property. They explained the risks (flipping is far riskier than cash flowing). Their real estate attorney explained that Esther was now the bank. No matter what happened, she would be paid first. If the flip failed, she could foreclose on the property and sell to get her money back. Esther was the mortgage note holder, and she was fully insured in case of fire or other disaster.

Rachel and Rick expected to sell the rehabbed property within four months, but told Esther it could take as long as six months.

In four and a half months the property was sold, and Esther made $3500 on her $100,000 loan. After investing on two more flips that year, Esther made more than 10 percent on the reinvested $100,000.

Nora and Lance K.—small business owners, spending a lot of time on their business and want to diversify their profits in to real estate

Nora and Lance are typical small-business owners expanding a successful company and working long hours...often not seeing each other except in passing, for days. Business is doing well, and after a recent expansion and additional employees they came to realize that they had been placing "all of their eggs in one basket"—their business. Although they were sure they "couldn't fail," there was always the nagging thought—the "what if." There had to be an exit strategy. They decided that reinvesting all of their hard-won wealth back into their company could be a risky maneuver. So, after hearing a REE present at a local business meeting, they decided that real estate was a great way to diversify.

They didn't want anything too risky, and preferred passive to active income for tax purposes, so on the advice of the REE they opted for the steady stream of passive income through long-term cash flow and returns in multifamily and commercial real estate. Within three years they had partnered with the REE on eight properties throughout the country, and now have a passive income stream of over $100,000 in addition to their business income. These eight properties also provide tax depreciation, and at sale should net them an additional profit to cushion their nest egg. They expect to continue investing as private money partners with the REE as more deals are made.

Jules S.—what happens when you overpromise and underperform!

Jules was sure he had hit the "mother lode." He had the perfect property and was eager to share with friends. He presented what appeared to be a can't-lose opportunity. It ticked all of his boxes: good area, brick building with pitched roofs, garden-style one- and two-bedroom units, stabilized, and low vacancy. All of the numbers fell into place. What Jules forgot was to stress test the property, or determine what really could go wrong under different scenarios. This is Rule #1 when evaluating a property. What Jules didn't realize was that a major employer in the area was moving, and because there were only a few major employers in the area (something Jules should have considered), this could affect his tenant base. This was a C-class property and most of the tenants were lower paid white-collar and blue-collar workers—many employed by the company that was moving away.

Of course, it's difficult to be prepared for every scenario, but understanding what can affect the occupancy of your building is important. Jules presented his property plan to his investors and "promised" that in five years they would double their money. This is not an outrageous claim—it is quite possible—but not generally something you want to promise.

Six months after the purchase of the property, the major employer began closing operations. As this happened, Jules began losing tenants, and new tenants didn't come as quickly. Within the first year, occupancy went from 97 percent to 85 percent, seriously affecting the ROI and passive income flow. By year two the vacancies were increasing, and Jules had to give concessions and lower rents to attract new tenants. By year three, things had stabilized because several small business had begun moving into the area and vacancies were declining. However, it took eight years, not five years, for the investors to get their 100 percent ROI. Private money partners were unhappy, and as a result several of them decided not to invest in Jules's next opportunity.

Lesson learned? REEs cannot predict the future...but it is better to under promise and over perform than vice versa. A savvy REE will stress-test a property to get the most likely outcome, and then be conservative with that result. As an investor you want to know the REE has considered all possibilities and has given you the most probable result. Please keep in mind that REEs can't predict the future, but they should consider the possibilities based on current and historical events.

Your story may be similar to one of these, or it may be unique. In each case, these private money partners knew *why* they wanted to invest (and not do the work). They put their money to work for them.

Chapter 11

A Final Word

There are three basic steps to making money as a private investor in real estate (after reading this book, of course).

1. Find a real estate entrepreneur (remember, they will often refer to themselves as real estate investors) by talking to friends and family, networking, and social media.
2. Interview and ask questions. Do your due diligence—you can never ask too many questions—to create a solid foundation of trust.
3. Create a solid relationship. This doesn't have to take a long time.

Then there are three expectations you should have as a private investor.

1. Expect the REE to be transparent.
2. Expect to be transparent with the REE.
3. Expect to make money!

Private investors desiring a regular income, with an optimal balance between risk and reward, generally will prefer real estate consisting of land, buildings, and fixed equipment. Moreover, the supply of land is limited and of fairly stable (though generally increasing) value. Real estate, therefore, is widely considered the best ultimate security and a solid basis for building lasting wealth.

Diversification

Not many real estate entrepreneurs can acquire apartments on their own. The major advantage of private investments is that it allows the private investor to join with others in acquiring a number of different properties in different markets. The combined strength of the properties in the pool provides a permanent stream of steady income that is virtually unaffected by variances in individual property vacancy rates or individual market fluctuations.

Operating Capital

It is well known that an investment's staying power is the single most important factor to building wealth. Yet the need for operating cash is often overlooked when inexperienced REEs buy real estate. Private investments assure that sufficient capital is available to give the investment the ability to withstand economic downturns or temporary shortfalls.

Independently Assessed

Ownership of real estate by way of a private investment does more than bring stability to a portfolio. It also relieves stress! Because the returns are based on the properties' actual revenues, rather than the ups and downs of the speculative markets, private money partners don't have to check their computer or the daily paper to see how their investments are doing.

Registered Retirement Savings Plan Eligibility

Private equity investments are 100 percent eligible as US content for registered portfolios that allow you to put the stabilizing, revenue-generating, and appreciating benefits of real estate ownership to work for you through a SELF-DIRECTED IRA.

Whether you already have a large real estate portfolio and just want to add something new, or you are looking to add real estate to your investment portfolio, it's time to think for yourself and question the routinely accepted traditional advice so many people blindly follow. It's time to discover which advice, information, and strategies work best for you.

We hope that this book has given you the needed insight to kick start your investing in real estate. Know that there are real estate entrepreneurs out there who are eager to talk to you about how being a private equity partner or debt partner can help you generate and preserve sustainable wealth in any economy.

We hope this book has given you a head start to understanding that scammers like Bernie Madoff may get a lot of press, but that by and large real estate entrepreneurs are honest, community-focused business owners.

"Inspirational" Quotes

Here are some of our favorite quotes by speaker and author Jim Rohn. We hope they prompt you to start on your private investing journey today!

"Formal education will make you a living; self-education will make you a fortune."

"Money is usually attracted, not pursued."

"Either you run the day or the day runs you."

"Time is more valuable than money. You can get more money, but you cannot get more time."

"The few who do are the envy of the many who only watch."

"It is not what happens that determines the major part of your future. What happens, happens to us all. It is what you do about what happens that counts."

"Wealth is not a matter of intelligence; it's a matter of inspiration."

Terms and Definitions

The following are some of the terms commonly used in real estate investing. We include them here so that you can familiarize yourself with them. Some of them have been used in this book, and many you will hear as you talk to real estate entrepreneurs.

Capitalization Rate (Cap Rate) is the net operating income (NOI) divided by either the property's contract purchase price or its fair market value.

Cash-on-Cash Return (CCR) is the net cash flow divided it by the initial investment (down payment and other equity). The calculation does not take into account the time value of money or change in the property's equity.

Cash-on-Cash Return with Equity Build-up modifies the cash-on-cash return calculation by adding the property's net change in equity for that year to the numerator and adding all previously generated equity to the denominator of the cash-on-cash return ratio. The formula calculates the return on the property equity (i.e., the return on the cash that is "tied up" in the property).

Closing Costs are expenses incurred by the buyer and seller in a real estate transaction over and above the price of the property.

Commitment Letter is a formal offer by a lender (bank or private investor) making explicit the terms under which it agrees to lend money to a borrower over a certain period of time.

Co-op is a multiunit housing complex where the residents own stock in the building instead of individual units.

Debt Coverage Ratio (DCR) is a property's net operating income divided by the amount of debt payments. Lenders use this calculation to determine the remaining operating cash flow after the debt payments.

Deed of Trust is a written instrument legally conveying property to a trustee often used to secure an obligation such as a mortgage or promissory note.

Depreciation is the decline in value of a property due to age, obsolescence, and other adverse changes that is deductible over a period of time on the income tax return. It can positively affect the return on investment for an investor.

Due Diligence or Property Condition report provides information on the financial and or physical condition of the property. This is typically used to help determine the cost of repairs or capital improvements that may be required.

Earnest Money Deposit (EMD) is a deposit made by a buyer toward the down payment to evidence good faith. Earnest money is typically held by the real estate broker or the escrow company.

Exit Strategy is the method by which the REE intends to exit or leave the investment property. The exit strategy is one of the first things the REE considers when analyzing a property. The REE may study multiple exit strategies based on location, condition, the operation, and the potential profits each exit may deliver.

Gross Rent Multiplier (GRM) is a property's fair market value divided by its gross rental income. This term is generally only used in commercial real estate value analysis and rarely used in multi-family real estate.

Internal Rate-of-Return (IRR) is the most widely used method of valuing a property's annual cash flow stream. Since a property's cash flow is earned in the future, those future dollars must be converted to present-day dollars. The IRR calculation discounts (reduces) the property's future cash flow at a rate (i.e., percentage) so that the sum of all cash flow for a specified time period is equal to the initial investment. The rate or percentage needed to do that is the IRR. In other words, IRR is the discount rate at which Net Present Value (NPV) is zero.

Joint Venture is an agreement between two or more parties that outlines the financial terms of their interaction, the role and duties of each party, and the intended outcome of the project they will be collectively working on.

Letter of Intent (LOI)—A letter of intent is a nonbinding agreement stating two or more parties' desire to enter into a real estate transaction, such as a sale or lease. The letter provides an outline of the proposed transaction so the parties can negotiate before committing to a contract. If any party is not satisfied with the terms, he can propose a counteroffer. If the counteroffer is accepted, the letter of intent is revised and reviewed again by all interested parties. Any party can decide against the deal at any time before the final sale contract or lease is signed.

Loan-to-Value Ratio (LTV) is the outstanding debt divided by the value of the property. This ratio is used to determine the amount of leverage and property equity. The debt balance can be the beginning or end-of-year balance. The property value used can be the contract price or the fair market value at the end of the year.

Modified Internal Rate-of-Return (MIRR) modifies the IRR to avoid the drawbacks of the traditional IRR. The IRR implicitly assumes that all cash flow is either reinvested or discounted at the computed IRR rate. In reality, a property's cash flow probably will not be reinvested at the computed IRR rate, but rather earn zero or a small amount of interest. The MIRR eliminates the reinvestment assumption by utilizing user-stipulated reinvestment and borrowing rates.

Mortgage Insurance Premium (MIP) Payments are insurance premiums charged by a lender to protect that lender against loss from a mortgager's default. The rates are charged on the balance of the loan and may be paid annually, monthly, or in some combination of the two (split premiums).

Net Operating Income (NOI) is a property's gross rental income reduced by all expenses except for loan payments, income taxes, mortgage insurance premium (MIP) payments, and sometimes funded reserves.

Net Present Value (NPV) converts future dollars into present-day dollars by discounting (reducing) the future cash flow of a property by a given rate or percentage. The initial investment (down payment) is subtracted from the discounted dollars to derive the NPV. A positive NPV means that the property will generate a higher return than the given rate or percentage used to calculate the NPV amount.

Operating Memorandum (OM) is the information package on a property for sale typically provided by the real estate broker. The package includes a review of the property, location, financials, pro forma, pictures, maps, and so forth that the buyer will need to make a first assessment and initial analysis of the deal.

Preferred Interest is the interest on the investment that is paid to the investor before any other payments from cash flow are paid out. Typically, preferred interest paid to investors continues as long as the property is owned by the REE.

Private Placement Memorandum (PPM) is basically a prospectus for shares in a private company, or equity in a real estate project, much like the sort received by an investor in a stock, mutual fund, or other publicly traded security. It details all of the terms of the investment, requirements of the investor, and proper disclaimers and disclosures related to the business and the equity.

Pro Forma refers to the possible future financial performance of the property. It may be based on historical performance as well as the performance of other properties in the same general location.

Proof of Funds is a statement by a bank or financial institution that a depositor has a certain amount on deposit. Similarly, a **proof of funds liquidity** provides evidence that the amount on deposit is accessible immediately or may provide a date of liquidity.

Purchase and Sales Agreement (PSA) is a legally binding contract between seller and purchaser for the sale and purchase of real estate. The terms of the agreement are mutually negotiated and ratified upon both parties signing the document.

Repositioning – A "repositioning" is a real estate investment strategy whereby the owner changes the financial position of the property in the market place. Economic value is added to the asset by changing the physical appearance, or the operations of the property which may subsequently increase profits when vacancies are decreased and rents are increased.

Return on Investment (ROI) is a performance measure used to evaluate the efficiency of an investment or to compare the efficiency of a number of different investments. To calculate ROI, the benefit (return) of an investment is divided by the cost of the investment; the result is expressed as a percentage or a ratio.

Seasoning in real estate usually refers to the length of time that a property owner has owned a particular property, known as title seasoning. Seasoning can also refer to the length of time a borrower has held a particular loan.

Securities and Exchange Commission (SEC) is a government commission created by Congress to regulate the securities markets and protect investors. In addition to regulation and protection, it also monitors the corporate takeovers in the United States The SEC is composed of five commissioners appointed by the US President and approved by the Senate. The statutes administered by the SEC are designed to promote full public disclosure and to protect the investing public against fraudulent and manipulative practices in the securities markets. Generally, most issues of securities offered in interstate commerce, through the mail or on the Internet, must be registered with the SEC.

Section 1031 is the section of the US Internal Revenue Service Code that allows investors to defer capital gains taxes on any exchange of like properties for business or investment purposes. Taxes on capital gains are not charged on the sale of a property if the money is being used to purchase another property; the payment of tax is deferred until property is sold with no reinvestment.

ABOUT THE AUTHORS

Anca Markie, founder and managing partner of Silver Lining Properties and Silver Lining Capital Partners has been an entrepreneur and business owner for over fourteen years.

Anca currently lives in Richmond, Virginia with her husband (and business partner) of 35 years.

When asked about how she views herself she offers her favorite quote: *I'm the woman that jumps out of bed every morning and when her feet hit the ground the devil wakes up and says "Oh, crap, she's up!"*

Silver Lining properties is a boutique real estate investment company whose primary investment strategy includes long-term buy-and-hold of 100- to 400-unit multifamily properties around the USA. Other strategies include single-family "flips" and buy-and-hold of storage facilities and office properties.

For additional information you can reach her at

anca@silverliningproperties.com or visit the websites

www.silverliningproperties.com

www.silverliningmoney.com

If you are interested in learning more about real estate investment opportunities with Silver Lining Properties, please contact her at anca@silverliningproperties.com

Caline Bruyn, founder and managing partner of Aurora Property Acquisition and Sound Venture Partners and has been an entrepreneur and business owner for over twenty-three years.

Caline currently lives in Bellingham, Washington with her husband (and business partner) of 36 years.

Aurora Property Acquisition is a real estate investment company based in the Puget Sound area of Washington. The primary focus niche includes single-family "flips" of properties that previous rehabbers neglected to complete. These undervalued and distressed properties receive a new lease on life through efficient, caring work by Caline and her team.

For addition information you can reach her at

caline@aurora-pa.com or visit the websites at

www.aurorapropertyacquisitions.com

www.sound-vp.com

If you are interested in learning more about real estate investment opportunities with Aurora Property Acquisition, please contact her at caline@aurora-pa.com

Share with Us

If you would like to share your thoughts about this book or your private investing experience with us, please go to our book website.

www.theprivateinvestorbook.com

Would you like to share this book with your friends and family? Learn how you can get books to share at a discount or FREE. Just go to www.theprivateinvestorbook.com and fill in the contact form.

We work with many real estate investors and private investors around the country. If you would like to be one of our partners or just learn more about what you need to do to become a private investor partner please contact us.